Praise for *Sport in Modern Irish Life*

'Take everything you think you know about sport, park it and enjoy wonderfully told stories through a completely unique lens. Brilliantly written and put together. This book gives us all a look at the present and the past through facts – and more importantly with its own unique take on important events. A must read.'

Oisín McConville

'It's incredible how perfectly told stories about what should seem a broad subject can feel so personal, not just to the author, but to the reader as well. So many disparate tales somehow fit together and evoke a full range of emotions. From grieving a lost Irish US Open tennis champion, to smiling at a hurling rivalry during the War of Independence, I learned so much – and felt so much – throughout.'

Joanne Cantwell

**Also by Paul Rouse**

*Sport & Ireland: A History*

*The Hurlers: The First All-Ireland Championship and
the Making of Modern Hurling*

# SPORT IN
# MODERN IRISH LIFE

PAUL ROUSE

MERRION
PRESS

First published in 2023 by
Merrion Press, an imprint of Irish Academic Press
10 George's Street
Newbridge
Co. Kildare
Ireland
www.irishacademicpress.ie

9781785374548 (Paper)
9781785374555 (Ebook)

A CIP catalogue record for this book is
available from the British Library.

Typeset in Sabon LT Std 11/17 pt

Cover design by Fiachra McCarthy

Irish Academic Press/Merrion Press is
a member of Publishing Ireland.

MIX
Paper | Supporting
responsible forestry
FSC
www.fsc.org    FSC® C021394

'The years run like leaves'

Catriona Clutterbuck,
'October' in *The Magpie and the Child* (2021)

# CONTENTS

# INTRODUCTION

Sport wraps itself around the emotions like bindweed. The meaning of sport lies in how it makes a person feel; sport which leaves you feeling nothing has no relevance. Even the most mundane of sporting events can provoke extravagant feelings – good and bad. These can somehow seem proportionate in the moment, even when they are clearly not at all so when viewed in hindsight. The story of any person's relationship with sport is unique unto themselves – it is the story of their own sporting world. But, in sport, the personal is also intimately connected with the universal; most sport is a shared experience even if not shared in precisely the same way.

There is a basic question that bears out the place of sport in modern life: what is it that people talk most about in the hours when they are not working or not sleeping? There is a very significant section of modern society for whom the answer to that question is sport. People who play sport are obviously the core of the modern sporting world, but playing is only the beginning of the matter. Those who are spectators or who buy sporting merchandise or who make their living in the multiple overlapping industries that are orientated to sport are also of fundamental importance. Modern sport would be an entirely different thing without this vast human hinterland.

People choose sport because of the happiness it brings them, and – often – this overwhelms everything else as a reason for sporting choice. The elemental joy of kicking or hitting or running or throwing is something that extends back in history across millennia. There is nothing in this world to replace that fundamental pleasure. That is not to say that there are no other pleasures that are as great – or even greater. It is merely to point out the particular nature of the pure fun of playing and the difference it can make to your life.

But the pursuit of pleasure and the happiness that comes from sport is not adequate as an explanation for why and how people partake in it. Sporting engagement is also shaped by the influence of where people live, or what they work at, or where they went to school, or what games their family and friends played, or how much money they have, or whether they are religious or politically active or are of a particular colour, gender or generation.

Which brings us back to the personal. This book is a personal exploration of sport. As well as the many essays and stories published here for the first time, others have evolved from articles written for the *Irish Examiner* and pieces recorded for RTÉ's *Sunday Miscellany*. They are the culmination of sporting experience as a player, manager, supporter, consumer, journalist and historian. They are an attempt to record, in the round, at least some of the sheer variety of experiences available in sport. And they are a reminder, too, that the wheel does not ever stop turning.

# 1 DREAMS

'I'm thirty-six years old, I love my family, I love baseball, and I'm about to become a farmer. But until I heard the voice, I'd never done a crazy thing, in my whole life,' says Ray Kinsella in the opening scene of *Field of Dreams*, a 1989 Hollywood blockbuster. That voice was saying, over and again, seven words that became a catchphrase that soon extended beyond sport: 'If you build it, he will come.' Kinsella (played by Kevin Costner) interprets the words as an instruction to build a baseball field on his newly bought farm. Despite the taunts that he is insane, supported by his wife Annie (Amy Madigan), Kinsella builds his field of dreams. Every night, the ghosts of Shoeless Joe Jackson and seven other Chicago White Sox players, banned from the game for throwing the 1919 World Series, wander out from between corn stalks and play baseball on that field. The film blends fantasy, myth and sport to tell a story that is about much more than dreams of baseball. It was panned by those critics who saw in it an exercise in manipulative sentimentality. But it is beloved of those who see it as magical and witty, a poignant exploration of loss and dreams of regaining, even briefly, what is gone.

Dreams are essential to sport; they encourage unlimited expectations for achievement. They fuel the ambitions of competition; they sustain loyalties even when fortunes might be at their lowest; they inspire. The idea of dreaming – and of dreams made real – is embedded in the language of sport. There is the Dream Team (the American Olympic basketball team of 1992), the Theatre of Dreams (the marketeers' rebranding of Old Trafford stadium), *Hoop Dreams* (the award-winning documentary), Dream Sports (the Indian sports technology company that includes in its holdings a platform for a fantasy sports league called Dream11). The list runs on and on, nuzzling into the lives of everyone with a significant interest in sport.

This dreaming is encouraged, even expected: the advice at every turn is to dream, to pursue those dreams and to do so without reserve, to never let them die. In the autumn of 2020, an unheralded outfielder with the Tampa Bay Rays, Brett Phillips, made a stunning, freakish walk-off hit, becoming the hero in the Rays' 7–6 victory over the Los Angeles Dodgers in Game 4 of the World Series of baseball. After the game, he was so filled with adrenaline and emotion that he needed to be put on a drip. When he recovered, he said: 'I definitely want to extend some advice to all the kids out there: keep dreaming big. These opportunities, they're closer than you think. They can come about. Just keep dreaming big, kids, of an opportunity like this, having an unrelenting belief that it will happen. And it does. Things like this happen.'

But there is an ambivalence to dreams in sport. A lifetime given over to the pursuit of a sporting dream can sour when that dream remains unfulfilled. The idea that every broken heart can be mended is not realistic. Even when dreams are lived, when a lifelong ambition is met, the fulfilment can often merely be fleeting. The yearning is to be back in the moment that has passed. Viewed from posterity, dreams can ache whether they are lived or unlived. But they ache more than anything, when the prospect of them being lived is gone, when the very act of playing has been lost. As Caitriona Lally wrote in *Eggshells*: 'When I wake the next morning, my dream is so close, I can smell the overripe fruit at the edge of it. It's a recurring dream about a bowl of fruit on the verge of rotting. Then I slap my head until the dream has faded and my head can only think of the pain.'

## New Boots

A new pair of football boots are sitting on a rack in a shop in the midlands. They're heavily discounted in the sales – discounted so far that I wonder what must be wrong with them. I don't play anymore, undone by age, so I wander on and leave them sitting snugly beside each other, a perfect pair. And then old habits take a hold and I wander back. I look at them for a little bit, as if standing in front of the Mona Lisa. I wonder, more than anything else, why it is I keep looking. It's not that I'm transfixed, more than I've been transported to another place and I'm beginning not really to think properly anymore.

So I pick up the boots. And I examine them. And they perform the miracle of becoming even more perfect. The stitching and the laces and the cut of the ankle, the run of the cogs beneath the sole, the way the flap sits down. I push my thumb against the insole and marvel at how light and soft everything seems. The boots have the feel of being more comfortable than worn slippers. Still, I move to put them back on the rack. Buying a new pair of football boots at my age makes no sense. Unless you're one of those freakish outliers who have denied time and social conventions and the decline of their own bodies to continue to play. I haven't managed that.

But then I make a mistake – I smell the boots.

From that moment it's over. The boots smell like Christmas morning and being a child and the unbridled joy of opening a box, knowing what's going to be in there, but being wild with excitement anyway. I smell away and it's intoxicating. But I keep my dignity – I'm not going to kiss the boots in public. I'm better than that. Not even a sneaky one. Maybe later, in the privacy of home. Or, more likely, when I get back to the car and open the box for a second time because the journey home will surely be impossible to make with the longing. I know already that I'll take them out of the box and put them on the passenger seat beside me for the drive home.

I tell the shop assistant that I'd like to try them on. She brings out the boots and leaves them in my hands. There's the trace of a smile on her face. I take out the paper that was nursed into the toe of the boots and sit there pushing the tops of the laces through the holes, making sure the length of lace on each crossing is exactly right. I love the fact that nobody has put their feet in these boots before now. Although I wish I'd better socks on. The lacing is done. A little pause. A shift of the body on the leather stool. Then the boots are on, one after the next time, first the left and then the right, as always. I stand up and flex into them and gently move.

It's pure bliss. They've been made only for me. I know I'm buying them now. I've known, of course, for a while now, definitely since I smelled them, but possibly even from when I saw them on the rack. All doubt has now been obliterated. I don't want these boots – I need them.

Then I hear a snort.

'You're not buying those boots, are you? For fuck sake! You must be fifty!'

'Howareya, haven't seen you in a while.'

'I'm grand. But what are you doing buying boots?'

And then I half-explain what's after happening – the glimpse, the walk away, the walk back, the feel of the boots, the smell, the urge to try them on. And I say, 'Sure, you know yourself …'

But he says, 'No. What would you want boots for?'

And then I remember what he was like when he played. How he never really could kick a ball without finding someone to run into first. And, even then, that he could kick it at all seemed at least a mild surprise. For fifteen minutes, the two of us stand chatting in the middle of the shop. The present is abandoned and, instead, it's back to the solace of the past: matches and fights and arguments and pints. I wallow in the nostalgia, ignoring the fact that we would gladly have poisoned each other for the best part of two decades.

All the time I'm standing there in a pair of football boots, perfectly laced-up, the black leather shaping itself around my feet in an embrace that could not be more natural. His sons come over and there are introductions. They're huge lads, but with the faces of teenagers still waiting to grow into themselves. I ask about school and football and then it ends in handshakes and good wishes.

As he turns away, he says with a smile to the boys: 'Come on, we may go. We better let this lad buy his boots.' The two sons stop, unsure what he's talking about. Then they look down and they see the football boots sticking out from under my jeans. I don't exactly blush, but I'm not looking forward to having to explain things again.

The lads are great, though – they're too sound to laugh out loud. Their mother must be some woman.

But I can see the laughter in their eyes. And the confusion. They couldn't see their own father in a pair of football boots and yet here's a man of his vintage buying a new pair. Off they go out of the shop and I can easily imagine the chat in the car.

Still, I sit back down on the leather stool and undo the boots. The shop assistant comes over and asks if I'm taking them. There's a silence. I think about making a joke about unscrewing the cogs and remaking them as slippers. But that would be a little bit pathetic. It's just a joy to be standing in a shop buying a pair of football boots.

Yet I hear myself say: 'No thanks.'

And that comes as a bit of a surprise. So I change my mind and go to say, *Actually, yes. I will.*

But the words don't come out. Instead, I hear myself say,

'No. Sorry – thanks. I'll leave it. They're perfect but they don't quite fit.'

## The Glorious Disease of Hope

Every January leaves men and women diseased with hope that this year will be their year. In this new dawn, the rawness of defeat can begin to be purged by those who have come up short and who now go again in search of glory. Dressing-rooms fill up with players and officials who are pulled back into an endeavour that will define much of the coming year. Some are pained at the prospect of the slog that awaits but just cannot bring themselves to stay away. Others simply love it all: they love the training, love the travelling, love the matches.

Almost everyone who stops playing misses the physical act of the game. They may understand that their body is no longer able or that their lives have swung in ways that lead them to walk away, but anyone who has ever played must miss the sheer fun of a happy dressing-room. There is nothing quite like the giddiness of such a dressing-room on the first night back in January. Even the most unlikely of potential victors – shots that are too distant merely to be called long ones – find something inside that hints at a new beginning. The overwhelming evidence that victory is so unlikely as to be essentially unthinkable is shifted around and reshaped to allow shafts of light split the darkness. Scenarios are imagined that end with men on other men's shoulders, cups being presented, a speech, bonfires, a wild night. Best of all – the Monday. Nothing beats the Monday after winning a championship: a day that begins early and lasts well into Tuesday, and maybe forgets to stop for another few days.

Reality won't be long about blowing all those joyous thoughts to little pieces, but much of the joy of sport is how it provides a platform for people to dream. This dreaming is not a simple matter of escapism, an attempt to beat down the walls of 'real life' and to find joy in an experience that exists outside normality. Sport is a normal part of everyday life. It is something people do and something they think about all the time. What makes it all the more powerful, however, is that it is also something they can imagine. It is this capacity of sport to make people dream, even as they do, that allows it grab such a hold on people's lives. For example, playing a game – any game – can bring pure joy. This is true of even the most seemingly banal of games.

The Bosnian novelist Aleksandar Hemon – who fled from Sarajevo in the midst of war in 1992 – wrote a lovely memoir of his life in which he talked about playing five-a-side soccer. He wrote of 'the rare moment of transcendence that might be familiar to those who play sports with other people; the moment, arising from the chaos of the game, when all your teammates occupy an ideal position on the field; the moment when the universe seems to be arranged by a meaningful will that is not yours; the moment that perishes – as moments tend to do – when you complete a pass. All you are left with is a vague, physical, orgasmic memory of the evanescent instant when you are completely connected with everything and everyone around you.'

Mostly – almost always – sport does not seem like this. Mostly five-a-side soccer is an hour spent panting like a thirsty sheepdog, swinging kicks at the ball or at another panting sheepdog. For all that there are dreams in sport, its reality is often laced with struggle, disappointment, rejection, disillusionment, even anger. Only a fool can argue that sport is something that is inherently, absolutely good. For example, people who look to sport to uphold notions of integrity and fair play are certain to be cruelly disappointed. Wilkie Collins, writing in the nineteenth century, said that far from teaching a man virtuous behaviour, sport instead taught him how 'to take every advantage of another man that his superior strength and superior cunning can suggest'. The sordid underbelly of modern sport – the cheating, fixing, drug-taking, violence, greed, exploitation and narcissism – is plain for all to see.

All of that is undeniable, and so too is the inevitability of defeat. Some defeats feel so bad that they can almost never be really shaken off. They wander across the mind at the most unexpected of moments and the pain returns. Telling someone that it is only a game and that losing a game is in no way important in the greater scheme of things, especially when set against the real problems of people's lives, is to state the obvious – but it is also to completely miss the point. The loss of proper perspective when it comes to sport sits at the very core of why it matters. Sport colonises the emotions and this – more than anything else – goes a long way to explaining the hope that January brings. It may be that a passion for play is at the heart of what attracts people to sport in the first place, but hoping and dreaming is often what brings them back again and again.

Because this is the year.

## New Year's Day, 2022

This year, I am to make my debut as a boxer.

My friend Murt has appointed himself as my coach. He has never boxed either, but being reared on a diet of *Rocky* films and Muhammad Ali television appearances means he feels well-placed to direct operations.

His main contribution so far has been to make elaborate plans for the production of a short film of my 'training camp'. This is to involve not merely footage of me sparring with a range of different opponents, but also me chopping wood and lifting boulders and displaying all manner of physical prowess in forests and mountains. He is a man for whom the aesthetic is everything.

Murt has also focused on writing lines that will allow me to perform at my best in the pre-fight taunting. 'The words matter,' he says. This is presumably why he also wants to get his friend, the poet, to act as corner man. The poet is a fella who once fainted in an opticians.

My opponent is a bigger man than me. He breakfasts well and brings this momentum with him through the day. He also 'did a bit of boxing' when he was younger. These two things give him what I think most people would consider a significant competitive advantage. Against that, when he tries to run, he looks like he's about to dislocate a shoulder.

So why are we fighting? The quick explanation is that my opponent returned to a bit of sparring recently to get fit and he loved it. A conversation started about this one evening. One line borrowed another and within a few minutes I had not just agreed to a fight, but had actually proposed it.

This seems sensible; I'm only fifty-one.

It's now more than thirty years since I first saw a real sporting fight. I'd a great view of it. Indeed, I was even a little bit responsible for it starting. In keeping with the etiquette of things, I should probably have been involved in it.

It was the early 1990s. I was just twenty years of age or so and had arrived in England on a Friday to look for work. Two days later I was playing a football match on a public park in Manchester.

The game was good fun, a leisurely introduction into the social life of the vast swathes of Irish people who lived in northern England. I was playing centre-forward and midway through the second half I took a shot from about forty yards. The ball only went about six feet wide. The umpire on the nearest post decided to put up the flag. He was not a neutral and was instead doing his duty by his club, as he saw it. After all, a well-chosen umpire is a vital member of any forward-line.

But on this occasion he may as well have fired a gun in the air to start a race. The first man to throw a punch at him was the goalkeeper. The two of them – umpire and goalkeeper – then ended up rolling around in the March muck.

This was just the start of things. Men appeared from everywhere and within seconds I was more or less the only player on the field not fighting. For a couple of minutes, the referee and myself stood beside each other as the fight spread out around us. He was nicely droll: 'I'm not sure Sunday morning is always the best time for a match.'

Normally, of course, these things are more push and posture than anything else, but there was a bit of real punching in this one. Then it ended all of a sudden, for no apparent reason, and the match continued without further fuss.

The sound of a punch landing stayed with me, however. It is a singular thing.

It was a sound that was back in my head last night when I spent thirty minutes out in the shed. I've hung a punchbag from a wooden beam using a heavy chain. It cranks and groans every time I hit it. It's a pleasing sound. And it is a pleasing feeling, also, to hit the bag. I know the drill from the videos I've watched and from YouTube: left and right, uppercuts and jabs, a few hooks, all the while moving the feet and bobbing and weaving.

There's no science to it, of course, the way I'm doing it. It's just slow-motion exercise, using muscles that had taken early retirement. In the first flush of enthusiasm for being back active once more, everything felt great.

Quickly, though, that has no longer proved to be the case.

This morning my arms hurt so much that I struggled to open a second Mars bar. There is also a pain across my shoulders that only Hercules might recognise after he managed to clean the Augean stables in a single day by diverting two rivers.

I now have to hold myself in new ways. Even getting up out of a chair is complicated.

Murt rings to give me an update on the planning. He tells me that he thinks I should enter the ring wearing a costume. He proposes that professorial robes would be one option. He thinks that my opponent would be so enraged by the professorial robes, 'especially if you wear the fancy furry cap with them', that he will lose all discipline and be vulnerable to counter-punching. He doesn't seem to hear me when I question the strategy of angering a man I'm about to fight and whether counter-punching is really effective if you're on the flat of your back.

He goes on to say that he'll bring a big-boom speaker to what he is now calling 'the event' and will use it to play out 'The Final Countdown' by Europe as I step through the ropes and dance around. Apparently, this would set the right tone. The word he kept using was 'ominous'.

The lyrics to the first verse of 'The Final Countdown' run:

'We're leaving together,
Yes, it's farewell.
And maybe we'll come back
To Earth, who can tell?
I guess there is no one to blame
We're leaving the ground
Will things ever be the same again?'

I told him that I had received a message this morning from my opponent who had asked: 'Do you have headgear?' He had followed this message up with another one that read: 'And 16oz gloves?'

I tell Murt this is clearly an attempt to intimidate me and that my opponent was playing mind-games already. Murt nodded wisely at me. He said: 'This is good. You're already at the paranoia stage. This is where a fighter goes when they're heading towards a big showdown.'

I think about getting a new coach.

There's a voice in my head telling me I need to hit the bag again now. I head out to the shed and put on the gloves. The dog is after eating most of the padding out of the left one. So I keep throwing rights.

Ten weeks is plenty of time to get fit. When Ali trained for his fights in his compound at Deer Lake in Pennsylvania, it was intended in the first instance as a place of solitude away from the bright lights of the city, where he concentrated on getting physically and mentally ready to fight.

It didn't exactly work out that way. One of his biographers Jonathan Eig described the place in the weeks before Ali fought Ken Norton in 1973 as being like a carnival, with a revolving door of celebrities and entertainers. In fact, there wasn't even a gate to the compound. All manner of people wandered in and out as they saw fit. It sounded like great fun.

Murt appears through my shed door. He is carrying a huge framed poster of Ali. Along the bottom of the poster, in large font, run the words: 'The fight is won or lost far away from witnesses – behind the lines, in the gym, and out there on the road, long before I dance under those lights.'

He says: 'Stand over there and I'll take a photo of you training.'

I hold the Ali poster in my gloves. I tuck myself in and push myself out, trying to reshape middle-age.

# 2 PLAY

**H**istory shows us that the world of sport has traditionally accommodated the tastes of all comers. People have always found ways to make sport out of the everyday. The sports they created were often specific to their region (even as variations of universal play) and were shaped by its geography. Traditionally, this play was most in evidence across the centuries in Ireland at festivals and on fair days. These were days of music, dance, drink, fighting and play. Hugely popular were dancing competitions for the prize of a cake: the prize was awarded not to the most aesthetic dancer, but to the one who lasted the longest. At Pulty in Co. Leitrim, there were various forms of stone-throwing and weightlifting activities. At Lough Owel in Co. Westmeath, the tradition of swimming horses in the lake endured into the late nineteenth century at least. Part of the thrill of this sport was the danger that attended it: horses unused to immersion were startled and prone to respond with terror, leaving only the most accomplished riders to survive.

There is also the tradition of fighting – either men fighting individually with cudgels and fists, or in units as part of a faction fight. By the second half of the nineteenth century it was a tradition that was bitterly condemned by the union of British state and Catholic church that despaired of the pastimes of the peasantry. Accordingly, they sought at every turn to suppress it – and largely succeeded. But faction fighting was remembered with fondness and apparently engaged in with huge enthusiasm. Many songs and stories celebrate such fights, including ones at Benaghlin in Co. Fermanagh where the annual gathering 'used to end by a challenge-fight with ash-plants or black-thorns between two rival sections'. Another example of this – and there are many from all over Ireland – comes from Galway, where, at Maumeen in the Maumturk Mountains, there were cudgel-contests between men, oiled by the poitín that was circulating freely.

Violence was only part of the story. At Mullyash in Co. Monaghan there was a long tradition of novelty games. These games included hitting a ball that was suspended aloft between two poles and climbing a greasy pole set in a pool of water. In parishes all around Ireland, from Mount Brandon in Kerry up to the Inishowen peninsula much fun revolved around activities such as leapfrog and other games that were well-known all across England. Indeed, the parallels with what was happening in rural England were obvious and the great example of this was the Cotswold Games. These Games – revived in the 1950s and still in existence – began in the 1620s. It was a great day out that drew people from all across the Cotswolds and beyond. The sporting aspect of the day fitted in around the carousing and featured such tremendous sports as 'shin-kicking'. In this sport, two contestants attempt to kick each other on the shin in order to force their opponent to the ground, or to make the opponent shout 'Sufficient'. This world of play lives on. The modern contestants in shin-kicking – who compete for a world championship where the finals draw thousands of people – are allowed only to wear soft shoes and are refereed in the modern way.

All across the world, alternative forms of play thrive; they are driven by the desires of people to have fun, of entrepreneurs to make money, and of civic societies to draw people to their areas. An enormous variety of popular pastimes lives and breathes beyond the suffocation of modern organised competitive sport. From tug-o'-war to churn-rolling, the passion for fun and for competition – mixed in whatever weightings as suit the individual – offers an infinity of experiences. And this infinity rests on a love of play that reaches deep into the unknowable past.

## On the Ice

It's five minutes into a fifty-five-minute ice-skating session and I'm lying in an impossible shape in the middle of the temporary ice-rink that has been built at the RDS in south Dublin. It's as if a woolly-hatted gorilla has fallen from a tree and achieved exceptional angles of rest. Except there's no rest. There's an Ice Marshall attempting to pull me back into an upright position and there are children whizzing past and their skates are close to my nose.

The first four minutes had been spent edging around the boards along the sides of the rink, as if I were Spider-Man heading home from the pub after putting in a solid evening on a high stool. Then, the first venture out away from the safety of timber brings a fall that challenged the boundaries of anatomical capacity. Apparently, it is not enough to have seen something on TV to make replicating it possible. The signs around the rink were good guidelines after all: 'This is an ice rink. It's quite likely you will fall! PLEASE NOTE THAT WE ARE NOT RESPONSIBLE FOR INJURIES SUSTAINED WHILE ICE SKATING.' There's also advice around using your 'common sense', not forming trains while skating, wearing helmets and pads, not playing tag, and being prudent around small children.

There is also a glimmer of hope in those same signs. It emanates from the piece of the sign that reads: 'Persons, who in the opinion of the Ice Marshals, represent a danger to themselves or others, will be asked to leave the rink and no refund will be offered.'

I wonder what more I'd have to do to be considered a danger to myself and to others?

Anyway – in a sort of secular miracle – everything settles down after a while. Bit by bit I get used to it and it becomes possible to do a lap without ending up prostrate. All around me people are getting used to the ice and learning to skate.

It begs the question as to why there is no permanent ice rink in Dublin. Surely there must be a market for it? And for the sports that are played on ice? After all, across modern history every time there has been a big freeze in Ireland, people head for any piece of frozen water that they think will hold them. It is a lure to do something different and there is no denying that there is a thrill to flying along on ice. This is a universal impulse: everywhere that there is seasonal ice and snow, it is 'winter sports' that dominate. The desire of humans to fit their sports into the geography and climate of their lives – and to use both geography and climate to enhance sporting opportunities – is repeatedly demonstrated. Ice rinks are the way these past traditions are squeezed into the modern world in defiance of geography.

## The Currach Races

'Inishbofin on a Sunday morning.
Sunlight, turfsmoke, seagulls, boatslip, diesel.'

So run Seamus Heaney's great lines from 'Seeing Things'. And, here, on this late Sunday morning, the currach races at the Inishbofin Maritime Festival are in full flow. There's a slow breeze blowing in around the ruin of the old Cromwellian barracks and across the harbour. More than a hundred people are on the new pier, with at least that many more again gathered along the harbour wall. Mick Conneely is playing the fiddle and Michael Cunnane – the chairman of the organising committee – is gathering together the crews for the next race. Out on the water, the men competing in the four-oared race have rounded the marker at the top of the course. Michael Joe O'Halloran is commentating across the PA system and is urging on the Inishbofin men competing against visiting teams from around Connemara. The strain of the pull and the splash of the water are framed by the beauty all around. Back to the left is Knock Hill with its A-frame house. Straight in front, the glorious sand of Port Beach rises into the headland. In the distance, beyond the entrance to the harbour, sits abandoned Inishark Island, its old stone houses growing back into the land. The race – and all the races on the day – are fiercely contested. Crews have travelled in from Carna and Carraroe, Rosmuc and Inishturk, and along the pier, conversations shift between Irish and English. The shouting of the crowd grows louder as the currachs push through the water and on by the pier. In the end, the Inishbofin men are beaten into second place and the silver cup will leave the island for the winter.

The following day I'm out in a currach. There are two of us rowing in the harbour. I've never done this before. The feel of the timber in my hands is odd. I can't keep a rhythm. The currach is bouncing on the waves, the wind a little higher than the day before. We're pulling against the tide, out towards the opening to the harbour. Around the corner is the Atlantic Ocean. There are a few spots of rain hitting the back of my neck. I'm useless at this, working hard but achieving nothing. But I stay at it – it's great to be able to say that I rowed a currach.

In the same way, I once rowed a racing scull on the canal in Tullamore, after a new rowing club had been formed in the 1980s. People from that club – people I know – went on to become Irish champions and to row at the Olympic Games. They started rowing on a man-made strip of water that runs through a midlands bog and ended up at the very highest levels of global sport; the absurdity of it is wonderful.

Once, I was asked which Olympic sport I would like to have competed in. That day on the canal came immediately to mind. It was, of course, a question so detached from reality that it was hard to properly entertain it. But then the dreams push in. So the answer I gave was that it would have to be the rowing and its perfect mixture of power and grace and timing.

As I was later to find in the currach, sculling was clearly not for me and the Olympics did not beckon. I was too small, too lacking in power, too uncoordinated, too erratic in timing, too interested in ballgames; that is to shorten the list to its bare bones.

Nonetheless, if things change, I think the way I'd like to row in the Olympics is in the quadruple sculling. Just me and my three brothers. Our role model would have to be the Australian rower Sally Robbins who lay back in the boat and stopped rowing in the last 300m of the final at the 2004 Olympic Games. She was an outstanding rower, but she stopped, just stopped in the heat of an Olympic final.

That's fine with me – it sets precedent. Depending on a favourable wind and tide, myself and my brothers could just drift home. A gentle wave to the crowd. Another bottle of Bulmers. A quick check to see if all four are still on board. Proud parents in the stands. Offaly jerseys everywhere. Storm the medal presentation. Savage homecoming. The Freedom of Tullamore bestowed. A memoir full of lies.

## The Rapids

'It's my favourite sport,' said Jess.

She was standing on the side of a mountain in the highlands of Scotland, wearing a wetsuit and a lifejacket and a helmet. 'When you're out there on the raft and the water pulls you along, it's just thrilling. There's nothing as good as whitewater rafting.' Behind Jess, the River Garry was, indeed, promising thrills. The press of the water as it surged down through Glen Garry and onwards towards the River Tummel brought an endless soundtrack of crash and gurgle.

The first sporting challenge was to get into the wetsuit. This was made more difficult by the fact that the small parking area was full of people talking and laughing and walking around. Who could have known that zipping yourself into a wetsuit could bring such humiliation? Or the encouragement of so many passing motorists?

In the minivan bringing the first-timers up the river to the start of the raft-ride, Jess was asked whether people fall in? 'Yes,' she said. That reality was probably obvious or understood by all in a theoretical way, but hearing it said out loud brought a quicker beat to the heart. The safety instructions issued on the river bank quickened that beat still further. Don't panic if you fall in. Hold onto the rope that rings the side of the raft and you'll be pulled back on board. In time. And if you lose grip of the rope, don't panic, just wait in the water and we'll throw you another rope. And if the raft flips and you end up trapped under it, don't panic, and try and push yourself down under the water and back out. And if you end up being thrown into the deep channel, down under the water, don't panic. And definitely don't breathe in. Apparently, many people who drown do so because the shock of the cold water when they are submerged draws them to open their lungs and fill them with water.

So don't panic, refloat and head for the shore.

There were instructions on how to paddle and how when the shout from Jess came to 'Get down', the thing to do was to hold the rope and crouch into the raft and wait until she called for something else to be done when the worst of the rapids were passed.

The River Garry is a dammed river. The dam is opened on Thursdays and Saturdays. This brings a still greater flow of water. Naturally, this was a Thursday and the water was gathering and swelling as we lifted the raft along a narrow bank and into a shallow pool. The section of the river where we were stepping into is deemed to be category 4. There are six categories of difficulty in whitewater rafting. The most dangerous category is 6 – these are rivers which are so dangerous they are basically not navigable. Huge waves, huge rocks, dramatic drops that bring a reasonably solid likelihood of serious injury. Or death.

The categories fall down to 1 – these are stretches of water which are so gentle you may as well bring the bubble bath. And category 4? Medium waves, medium rocks, and demanding of sharp manoeuvres to stay afloat.

These categories are set out by the International Rafting Association, which organises competitive whitewater rafting competitions, culminating in a world championship. The sport has become increasingly popular since the decades immediately after World War II. It demands teamwork and initiative to guide the inflatable raft (between three and four metres long) down a river. In northern Europe, in April, it also demands a capacity to cope with the cold.

The sharp blast of cold when first stepping into the River Garry was intense. Then it was out of the water and into the raft. A brief paddle around a shallow inlet to confirm the instructions and practice paddling in unison. And it was out into the white water. Six of us on a raft. With six paddles.

Immediately, the water splashed up over the side of the boat and it was freezing again. And absolutely unnerving. Jess was shrieking with happiness, sending out instructions on what to do:

'Paddle forwards.'

'PADDLE FORWARDS!'

'Go left!'

'GO LEFT!'

'That's not left!'

She told us that we were about to come to the first serious stretch. Here, the river was falling away quickly, across huge boulders. It was darker, too. There were high birch trees and tall firs on the left bank. On the right bank, row after row of native Caledonian Spruces punctured the clouds. In the middle distance, a couple of chainsaws roared away.

'GET DOWN!' she shouted. 'GET DOWN!'

Down it was, crouched into the raft as it lurched and spun and bounced. There was water everywhere. A cold jet shot into the chest and the face. Everything was now wet. People were laughing and screaming and nobody else seemed to be panicking. Through the first section, a quick count saw we had lost nobody. Then it was through the second section, then the third, and on down to the end of the course.

All the clichés apply – it was utterly exhilarating, thrilling, spectacular, frighteningly brilliant.

But, best of all, it was over.

Except it wasn't. It was back into the minivan, back up the glen, back to the bank, back in the raft and back down the river.

This time it was different. There were a dozen kayakers coming down around us. They were being trained as instructors. They were part of a university course that is helping to transform the 'adventure sports sector' and helping, also, to bring a renewed sense of life to towns such as Fort William. All winter, this beautiful area is home to hundreds of students who come to take a course in Adventure Tourism at the University of the Highlands and Islands. They learn about adventure sports and running a business and minding customers and about the ways of bringing new dimensions of learning to people who are in a raft for the first time.

So it was now that on that second run down the river we turned the raft and paddled furiously back up into the worst of the rapids. There was a purpose to this. A change on the river bed, and the presence of slower moving water, kicked up the water that was flowing rapidly across the rocks. This broke its normal flow and caused it to ramp up to make a wave. This wave folded back on itself, and by putting the raft on top of it, we were able to surf. On the top of the wave it felt like we were flying along the river – but in reality we were going nowhere. It was a stunning way to finish.

Only one man fell out of the raft. It was on the second trip. He didn't panic. He got cold. Very cold. He didn't breathe in huge gulps of water. He held onto the rope and was pulled back into the boat. He loved it.

# 3 HILLSBOROUGH

On 15 April 1989, in homes and in pubs all across Ireland, people sat down to watch Liverpool play Nottingham Forest in the semi-final of the FA Cup. It was a fine spring afternoon, not ordinarily one for sitting in front of the television. But this was different: the number of live soccer matches shown on television that year in Ireland could more or less be counted on the fingers of one hand. So this was a rare treat: Liverpool against Nottingham Forest at Hillsborough stadium in Sheffield. It promised to be brilliant – and RTÉ had it live. There is no disguising the truth that this live broadcast of a football match became a live broadcast of mass death. More than three decades later, the events of this day have not brought a reckoning for those whose actions were responsible for the deaths of ninety-seven people. The torrents of grief that flowed through the lives of those who lost their family and friends, the guilt felt by many who survived, the mental anguish and misery, the raw pain of loss and suffering that were the inevitable outcome of such an event are incomprehensible in themselves. That this was accompanied by the police indulging in an orgy of vile slurs of those who died and those who survived is simply disgusting and reveals the absence of the most basic qualities of humanity. The scale of the cover-up is scarcely credible – and so too is its fundamental cruelty.

When it comes down to it, this story is all about class and power. The culture of perjury, brutality and callous disregard for the lives of ordinary people which defined the South Yorkshire Police was already well-practiced by the time the events of Hillsborough unfolded. It was a culture that had been revealed, for example, in the response to the miners' strikes of the early 1980s where excessive police violence in dealing with the strikes mixed freely with a willingness to commit perjury and the absence of basic ethical probity. There is no doubt that senior police officers in the force saw themselves to be untouchable. More than that, they clearly considered that the dishing out of beatings to miners was a form of natural justice – the miners were getting what they deserved and the notion that a striking miner may, too, have had rights was neatly dismissed. In itself, this was a perfect reflection of the political culture of England in the 1980s. And it found its perfect cheerleaders all across the Tory press.

The visit of Margaret Thatcher to Hillsborough after the tragedy, and the manner in which she – and her odious acolytes – were all too willing to accept the police version of events, was as predictable as it was shameful. That unity of the police, *The Sun* newspaper and Thatcher speaks volumes for the type of society which the Tories wished for and which they sought to create by their policies. The echoes of their righteousness, and of their contempt for the type of people which they imagined Liverpool fans to be, can still be heard today.

## The Match
### 2.59pm–3pm:

> *Brendan O'Reilly, RTÉ Studios: 'From Hillsborough, live and exclusive to Sports Stadium. Let's join our commentator George Hamilton, with Johnny Giles.'*

> *George Hamilton: 'Welcome to Hillsborough. The sun has come out to greet you ... And the match is on, with Liverpool in red playing from left to right. Forest in their changed strip of all-white.'*

The first cheer of the match comes in the second minute when the brilliant defender, Alan Hansen, receives the ball in the middle of the field.

Hansen has been out injured since suffering a knee injury in a pre-season match. He plays the ball out left to his central defensive partner, Gary Ablett. Ablett is caught in possession, however, by Nigel Clough and Forest force a corner.

This first corner leads to a second and as the camera pans across the penalty area, you can see the mayhem on the terrace behind the goal at the Leppings Lane end. There are already people trying to climb the huge steel fence that holds Liverpool fans in their terrace pens.

### 3.02pm:

> *John Giles: 'It's a big gamble, I should imagine, by Kenny Dalglish to play Alan Hansen. He's a great player, probably the best central defender in the country when he is fit. But it's his first game of the season and*

*in such an important match. I hope it comes good for him, because he deserves to do well.'*

The play is now mostly down the far end of the field, or around the middle. There's Ronnie Whelan and Ray Houghton and Steve Staunton mixing it with Stuart Pearce and Neal Webb and Steve Hodge.

Occasionally the ball strays towards Bruce Grobbelaar in the Liverpool goal. Behind the goal, you can see more and more Liverpool fans climb the fences – there are now dozens behind the goal.

When the game is in its fifth minute, the TV director leaves the action and switches to a camera which shows a close-up of what is happening behind Grobbelaar's goal. There is a clear crush behind the goals, something George Hamilton notes in his commentary.

The ball sweeps to the far end and Peter Beardsley hits the crossbar with a volley. The ball is cleared to the far end – where Liverpool fans are now on the pitch.

**3.06pm:**

*George Hamilton: 'And the police are on the pitch to tell the referee to stop proceedings because there is a danger here that the crowd is going to encroach onto the pitch because of overcrowding at the back of the goal.'*

The referee, Ray Lewis, taps Ronnie Whelan on his lower back and says something. The players are being called off the pitch. A supporter grabs Steve Nichol, the Liverpool defender and points to the terrace and tells him what is happening.

The cameras show Graham Kelly, the secretary of the FA, walking on the pitch. Then other cameras show two Liverpool fans, men in their twenties, hugging each other and crying. And then there is a young man on the ground, clearly seriously ill, and police are tending to him as he lies, stretched out, in the penalty area.

**3.07pm:**

> *John Giles: 'There shouldn't be overcrowding. If the tickets were distributed and allocated properly, there shouldn't be overcrowding like this, should there?'*

> *George Hamilton: 'It's quite obvious there that some of these fans have been injured in the crush behind the goal ... And still the crowd sways; it's a very dangerous situation.'*

> *John Giles: 'They're not out of trouble there by any means ... I wouldn't like to be in that crowd, that's for sure.'*

> *George Hamilton: 'This is a situation fraught with danger. Crowds are corralled these days in football stadia and if there is any pressure on from the crowd behind, there is simply nowhere for those at the front to go.'*

The cameras now show people being pulled out over the fence, people being pulled out of the crowd to the upper deck, people falling to the ground.

There are two dozen police on the pitch now, walking from the Forest end to the Liverpool end, headed towards the crush.

There are already a few policemen on the high steel fence, standing looking into the crowd. They stand on that fence beside Liverpool fans. They are facing back into the crush, gesticulating frantically, police and fans trying to get the crowd to move back up the terrace.

But the crowd cannot go anywhere except forward.

### 3.09pm:

*John Giles: 'There's a lot of pressure on the front there. You'll find there'll be a lot of kids do go to the front to get a good view of the match. And they'll be in serious trouble at the front there.'*

*George Hamilton: 'It certainly seems like something has gone very seriously wrong in that terrace.'*

More and more people are now lying on the pitch. A first person is on a stretcher. Fans are still being pulled over the fence and pulled into the upper deck. There are scenes of panic and dismay and mayhem.

A father gets up off the grass, holding the hand of his young son – a boy of maybe seven years of age. The father is bewildered and the son is shocked.

A young male is put in the recovery position.

**3.14pm:**

> *John Giles: 'I certainly wouldn't like anyone belonging to me to be in that crush.'*

> *George Hamilton: 'There will be serious questions asked about this afterwards. That was a situation that should never have developed.'*

An ambulance screams along in front of the stand and down to the terrace.

A man takes a jumper and makes a pillow out of it for his friend, who is stretched on the grass and in considerable difficulty. He lays his friend's head on the pillow.

Somebody is trying to give CPR to another person on the pitch.

More members of the South Yorkshire police make their way across the grass. A long black line snakes along the far sideline.

Across the pitch, fans are trying to resuscitate other fans. Makeshift stretchers are being used to carry people away.

A second ambulance arrives.

George Hamilton hands back to Brendan O'Reilly in the studio in Dublin. Shortly afterwards, the programme returns to Hillsborough and live pictures are shown of people who have been crushed.

By now the scenes are of absolute carnage. People are motionless on the ground. There are frantic attempts to revive others.

This is a day like no other.

## The Never-ending Day

There are people for whom that day, 15 April 1989, the day Liverpool played Nottingham Forest in the semi-final of FA Cup, has never ended.

It never ended, most brutally, for the ninety-seven people who ultimately lost their lives at a soccer match. And it has never ended for their families, who have fought for justice for more than thirty years now.

In November 2019, the trial of the former South Yorkshire police chief superintendent David Duckenfield, for manslaughter, led to a 'not guilty' verdict. The outrage provoked by this verdict has been raw and deeply wounding.

It was manifest when Christine Burke, whose father, Henry, died at Hillsborough, stood up in court after the verdict and said to the judge: 'I want to know who is responsible for the death of my father, because somebody was.'

The judge – Sir Peter Openshaw – offered no reply.

A short while later, Margaret Aspinall, chairperson of the Hillsborough Family Support Group, whose son James, eighteen, was one of those who died, said simply: 'I blame a system that's so morally wrong within this country, that's a disgrace to this nation.'

The outpouring of grief and anger after the November 2019 verdict was made all the more stark because of the events of the last decade. After a long campaign for justice, families of the dead had succeeded in 2012 in having the verdict of 'accidental death' from the original 1991 inquest quashed.

This verdict was so reviled that there were families who had declined to accept the death certificates of those they had lost.

A new inquest was ordered. This inquest – which ended in 2016 – deemed that the ninety-six Liverpool fans who died at Hillsborough had been 'unlawfully killed'. (This figure was subsequently updated to ninety-seven, following the death of Andrew Devine in 2021. Andrew suffered life-altering injuries at Hillsborough.)

Crucially, it also deemed that no behaviour of Liverpool supporters had contributed to the disaster.

A central aspect of that inquest had been the unravelling of David Duckenfield. In the course of his evidence to the inquest, Duckenfield had admitted multiple failures in his handling of the match. These failures were manifest at every level – from his basic knowledge of the stadium, to how he prepared for the day and on to his handling of events around 3pm.

By the end of his evidence, under questioning from his own barrister, Duckenfield had agreed with the statement that his 'professional failings led to the deaths of ninety-six innocent men, women and children'.

The verdict of the inquest had prompted the Crown Prosecution Service to bring a prosecution that Duckenfield was 'culpable of gross negligence manslaughter'.

A first trial on this charge had resulted in the retrial which concluded in November 2019. At both trials, recordings of what Duckenfield had admitted to were played to the court.

But his barrister argued that those admissions were being taken 'out of context' and were the product of days of arduous questioning. The court was told that there were other issues that mattered also.

It was said that other officers on the ground should have acted more decisively, that their own initiative should have brought them to intervene, that the design of Hillsborough was at fault, that the crushing was not foreseeable, that Duckenfield was – in effect – a scapegoat.

Among those whom were blamed, anew, were Liverpool supporters; the allegations that supporters had misbehaved were raised again.

Duckenfield was exonerated by the court.

## Truth and Lies

Where can the truth of what happened on that April Saturday afternoon be found? How did this truth become so obscured? Where is justice to be found?

### 3.15pm:

> George Hamilton: 'In fact, John, the word has just come through as to precisely what the problem was. There was a gate broken – one of the exit gates was broken which enabled fans without tickets to gain access to the terrace. And that is the precise cause of the problem.'

This was a fiction – although at the time George Hamilton could not have known it. Indeed, in the context of the hooliganism of the 1980s and in the aftermath of the Heysel Stadium disaster, the words he spoke were eminently reasonable, particularly given the fact that the source of the story was the highest levels of the South Yorkshire Police.

Hamilton's commentary (and that of John Giles) during those minutes when – live on air – it became clear there was a serious problem in the terrace was restrained and, indeed, in the circumstances, it was remarkable; the sense presented throughout is of something having gone badly wrong in terms of crowd control.

Because, of course, the fans did not break down the gates. Instead, the gates were opened by policemen who were acting on the instructions of the South Yorkshire Police match commander, David Duckenfield.

As David Conn has written in his magisterial reporting which stretches back across the decades on this story, Duckenfield admitted at the inquest in 2016 'that he told a "terrible lie" even as the disaster was happening, falsely blaming Liverpool supporters for forcing open a gate and rushing in. That false account began years in which South Yorkshire police officers blamed the victims, rather than their own mismanagement, for the disaster.'

With people dying on the field, Duckenfield told the FA chief executive, Graham Kelly, that Liverpool supporters had rushed in through a gate they had broken open.

It was a lie which had actually been exposed in 1989 when a public inquiry was established. That inquiry had produced an interim report which was authored by Lord Justice Taylor, who recorded that David Duckenfield had ordered a large exit gate to be opened to alleviate a crush that was developing outside the Leppings Lane turnstiles.

Some 2,000 people poured in through the opened gate. Many of those people headed straight down a tunnel that was facing them. They came out of that tunnel straight into the crowded central sections of the terrace.

It was in these sections – pens 3 and 4 – that the crush of people turned lethal, eventually killing ninety-seven people.

Following on from the lie told by Duckenfield about the broken gate, senior police officers issued further lies, ones that are among the most notorious in modern British history.

These lies painted pictures of drunken, violent fans. The lies were published in *The Sun* newspaper in the week after the game, under the headline, 'THE TRUTH'. The lies told of fans robbing from victims by picking their pockets, of fans urinating on police officers, of fans beating up a policeman who was giving the kiss of life to a dying man.

When the 2016 inquest declared that no behaviour of Liverpool supporters had contributed to the disaster, it was a hugely important moment. As the families emerged onto the steps of Warrington court after that inquest, they broke into a spontaneous rendition of 'You'll Never Walk Alone'.

You do not have to be a supporter of Liverpool to be deeply moved when you look at that footage. Gathered together are parents and children and siblings of those who died. Some are wiping their eyes as they sing out the words with raw emotion. Others are embracing and still more pointing to the sky.

They had spent too many years fighting for the rights of their loved ones. Down at the far end of the court steps, a man stands swaying with a large red scarf held high over his head. On the scarf is the mythical Liver bird and, in huge letters, white-on-red, the word: JUSTICE.

But, in the aftermath of the November 2019 verdict which found Duckenfield not guilty, what can that word mean?

# 4 ART

When the art critic and historian Robert Hughes published his guide to Barcelona in 1992, the *New York Times* wrote that the book was destined to be a classic. Hughes wrote beautifully about the art and architecture of the city, of its history and culture, and of the people who made it what it is. But there is a jagged hole in the middle of the book: there is nothing (absolutely nothing) about Barcelona FC and its importance to the life of the city, except for a fleeting reference to 'the football ground' to the west of the city. Hughes's *Barcelona* is a book that has Gaudí as its central figure. That is understandable. There are many cities with football clubs and none with a Gaudí; his masterpiece, the Sagrada Familia cathedral, may be incomplete, but is almost better for that and his genius is fundamental to the wonder of the city. Yet, it is incomprehensible that a book on Barcelona should ignore its premier football club. How can any study of the culture and identity of the city not include Barcelona FC?

It is as if, for Hughes, sport and art are distinct. It is true that he subsequently wrote a nice book on fishing, but – again – it was written in the context of a love of art. More interestingly, in his memoir *Things I Didn't Know* (2006), Hughes set out his view on sport in a more nuanced way. He acknowledged that he was never keen on watching sport, that he didn't care which team won a contest. He remembered from his schooldays in Australia his loathing of playing rugby, that watching it was almost as bad, and that rowing induced in him a coma. As an adult he had been to one horse race meeting in Australia and one baseball game in America, but had interest in neither. He said he enjoyed playing golf for a while, but nothing more.

More importantly, Hughes used sport to explain his approach to culture. He wrote: 'For of course I am completely an elitist, in the cultural but emphatically not the social sense. I prefer the good to the bad, the articulate to the mumbling, the aesthetically developed to the merely primitive, and full to partial consciousness. ... I don't think stupid or ill-read people are as good to be with as wise and fully literate ones.' He continued by noting that as a cultural critic, it was his job to distinguish the good from the bad, and – in other words – to be elitist. In answer to those people who criticised his disregard of sport, he said: 'I am no democrat in the field of the arts, the only area – other than sports – in which human inequality can be displayed and celebrated without doing social harm.' He continued: 'Australians have no difficulty with elitism in sports. On the contrary, it fuels their imaginations, it blots up their leisure time, and they prize it as their chief claim to national distinction. ... Competitive sports is not just an example, but the very essence, of elitist activity: by its nature, a competition can yield only one winner as against any number of losers. But if the harmless culture elitist is not a sports elitist, and unwisely confesses that he doesn't care who wins what at any Olympic Games, then woe betide him.'

Hughes put his case very nicely, but what he never managed to do was to link sport and art in any meaningful way. Nonetheless, there is a deep shared history between sport and art. Sporting art most usually focused, before the modern era, on hunting, shooting and fishing. There was also extensive equestrian art and, in the nineteenth century, portraits of famous boxers and runners. All of these sports, joined by cricket and golf, maintained a strong tradition of artistic representation. There were also celebrated paintings related to the various football games and to other modern sports such as baseball. Most usually, though, the imagery of sport found a more popular and ephemeral representation. Photographs in newspapers and magazines, cigarette and chewing gum cards, and the iconography of all manner of sporting mementos overwhelmed traditional representations in art.

But that does not mean that such art did not continue to be made, or that it had no value. From the portraits of sumo wrestlers in the Metropolitan Museum of Art in New York to the portrait of the English soccer international Tom Finney that hung in the National Portrait Gallery in London, paintings offer a vivid insight into modern sporting culture. As a representation of the sporting culture of celebrity in the 1970s, nothing quite matches Andy Warhol's 'The Athletes'. Produced in acrylic and silkscreen on canvas, between 1977 and 1979, Warhol's portraits of ten of the greatest sports stars of that decade – Muhammad Ali, Chris Evert, O.J.

Simpson, Dorothy Hamill, Kareem Abdul-Jabbar, Pelé, Vitas Gerulaitis, Tom Seaver, Jack Nicklaus and Willie Shoemaker – were completed by a man who had no interest in sport, but who understood its centrality to modern culture. You don't have to like sport to know that.

## Football is Art

When you walk around the National Football Museum in Manchester, you see many of the type of things that you would expect to see in any museum. There are artefacts and memorabilia and panels of text that seek to recall the past. There are stories of great players, great games and great clubs, a section which seeks to document the match-day experience, a history of grounds, the history of the way soccer has developed since its invention in 1863. Among the most striking exhibits are an English international jersey from 1872, the ball from the 1966 World Cup final, and some of George Best's clothes. There is the now obligatory area where you can demonstrate your own genius at kicking a football in the right direction.

This year there has been an exhibition on in the National Football Museum that is entirely different to anything that has gone before. Up on an upper floor, the 'Football is Art' exhibition is an extraordinary collection about the relationship between soccer and art. On superficial observation, soccer and art would not seem to make for easy bedfellows. This sense is acknowledged in the exhibition with a huge blown-up quote, high on its walls, carrying the words of John Gregory, the ex-Aston Villa and Derby manager. Gregory once said: 'What the fuck is art? A picture of a bottle of sour milk lying next to a smelly old jumper? To me it's a load of shit. I'd say football is art.'

Taking its name from the last three words of that quote, this exhibition reveals the sheer scale of the art that has sought over the last 100 years to explore the emotions that are provoked by soccer. This exploration is focused on a basic question: 'Can art in all its forms truly capture the emotions of a match?'

The attempt to answer that question ranges across more than seventy artworks and sculptures which show how generations of artists have depicted soccer. The works of art are grouped into different emotions: anticipation, devotion, relief, admiration, pride, belonging, nostalgia, joy and – of course – despair. What would sport be without despair?

Many of the pieces in the collection were on display for the first time and together they constituted the biggest exhibition on the relationship between soccer and art that had ever been put together. Household names and hidden gems hung side-by-side. Among the names of the painters on display were David Hockney, Banksy and L.S. Lowry.

Hockney's 'A Bounce for Bradford' is fantastic, depicting a football bouncing around, leaving lines and shadows in its wake. This was a print made in 1987. There were then some 30,000 people unemployed in Bradford and a local marketing campaign sought to fight back against the devastation wrought by Thatcherite policies in England's industrial towns. David Hockney was then living in Los Angeles and immediately lent his support once he heard of the campaign. His print was published in the local *Telegraph and Argus* newspaper as part of a supplement. A further 10,000 copies were then sold at a Royal Academy summer exhibition, all at the price of 18p, the original cost of the newspaper.

A more traditional painting is 'Going to the Match', by L.S. Lowry. It shows the outside of a football stadium before kick-off. Hundreds of supporters are hurrying toward the turnstiles, pouring out from terraced houses and factories, whose chimneys form the background of the picture. This painting – a classic evocation of the traditions of English soccer – was bought by the Professional Footballers Association for some £2 million. It is usually displayed in the Lowry Centre and has been valued as being worth up to £10m.

Also intriguing is Banksy's 'Football Terrorist' – this is now privately owned and was put on public display in England in this exhibition for the first time. It had previously been displayed as part of the 'War, Capitalism and Freedom' exhibition in Rome in 2016. It is one of the graffiti artist's most iconic works.

But this exhibition is much more than just the work of the famous few. It also includes work by many lesser known artists. For example, David Clarke's contribution, a portrait entitled 'Not a Penny More', can be found in the 'Despair' section of the exhibition. It shows a Blackpool FC supporter in anguish at the manner in which the fate of his club continues to spiral downwards. More than any photograph or piece of writing of what has happened to Blackpool in recent years, this portrait captures just what a club can mean to its supporters.

Even the making of the exhibition created its own stories. The painter Karel Lek submitted 'Football Spectators in Rain' for a 1953 competition. Afterwards he rolled the painting up and put it in a drawer. It remained there for almost seven decades until a copy of it was seen in a catalogue by a researcher at the National Football Museum. The researcher traced Lek and offered to acquire the painting.

A unique aspect of the exhibition is a section put together by students of fashion design and technology from the Manchester Fashion Institute at Manchester Metropolitan University. The students were asked to base a sportswear design on a piece of artwork from the collection – and what they produced was worth the visit in itself.

The last word on the matter should go to Arsene Wenger, the former Arsenal manager: 'Football is an art, like dancing is an art – but only when it's well done does it become an art.' This exhibition demonstrated just how enthralling the art of football can be when it is done well.

## The Hugh Lane

You can find hurling in the most unexpected places.

At one end of Parnell Square in Dublin – the end closest to Dorset Street – stands Charlemont House. It was built in 1765 and its limestone-clad and curved walls are majestic. The building is a legacy of James Caulfield, 1st Earl of Charlemont, and its design is an expression of his interest in the classical arts – something he developed when as an eighteen-year-old he undertook a grand tour of Europe in 1746.

Since 1933, this old townhouse has served as the permanent home of the Dublin City Gallery: The Hugh Lane. It houses a magnificent collection of art. This collection would be all the better, of course, if the National Gallery in London did not hold paintings – including masterly works by Renoir and Monet – which should by rights hang in Dublin. This is a tawdry story: in 1913, when plans to build a municipal gallery in Dublin collapsed, Hugh Lane gave to the National Gallery in London thirty-nine paintings which he had earlier planned to exhibit in Dublin. In 1915 Lane changed his mind and in a codicil to his will said that the paintings should be returned to Dublin should a suitable gallery be built to hold them.

But then Lane died when the Lusitania was torpedoed by a German submarine. His will had not been witnessed, even though initialled on every page, and the National Gallery in London did precisely what imperialists do – they declined to return the paintings. This, of course, is devoid of all integrity. But it is not surprising – naturally, the view from London would be that the paintings would be lost on the natives.

Either ways, what is undeniable is that the Hugh Lane Gallery on Parnell Square is now a magnificent place to visit, something that is worthy of a capital city. And it is free to enter. If you walk in through the main hall and cross through the exhibiting rooms, you can quickly forget that you are in a busy city.

There is a real pleasure in squeezing into the viewing space and looking into the remade studio of Francis Bacon. Beyond that, in a beautiful room, hangs the greatest painting associated with the game of hurling: 'The Tipperary Hurler' by Seán Keating.

For more than seventy years, Keating worked as an artist, an art teacher, and a broadcaster. His working life spanned the establishment of the Irish Free State and the story of his paintings – and much else – can also be found in Éimear O'Connor's fine book *Seán Keating: Art, Politics and Building the Irish Nation*. Among his famous paintings depicting the revolutionary era is his 1921 'Men of the South', which shows a group of IRA men gathering to ambush British soldiers. Indeed, it is said that 'Men of the South' is based mainly on photographs which Keating took of Seán Moylan's North Cork Brigade of the IRA – it hangs in the Crawford Art Gallery in Cork.

For its part, the 'Tipperary Hurler' painting was finished in 1928 and was completed for exhibition at the Amsterdam Olympics of 1928. At that time, art and poetry and music were an essential part of the Olympic programme. Keating did not win a medal, but the painting was eventually donated to the Hugh Lane Gallery in 1956 by an American called Patric Farrell, who was the curator of an art gallery in New York.

It is actually based on sketches completed earlier in the 1920s on John Joe Hayes, one of the stars of Tipperary hurling of the era. Keating had sketched Hayes playing in a match in Croke Park, possibly the 1925 All-Ireland final. The thing is, though, that there is more to the story of 'The Tipperary Hurler' than it being merely a rendering of John Joe Hayes, celebrated and all though he was.

In the months before the Amsterdam Olympics, Keating asked one of his students at the Dublin Metropolitan School of Art, Ben O'Hickey, to model for him. O'Hickey is reported to have born an uncanny likeness to Hayes – and his own backstory is a fascinating one.

Originally from Bansha in Co. Tipperary, O'Hickey had been a ferocious member – and then a leader – of the IRA in Tipperary. He had been imprisoned several times, in both Ireland and England, for his IRA activities. Once, down in Clonmel, when the War of Independence was gathering momentum, Ben O'Hickey was arrested by the Royal Irish Constabulary. A crowd heard of the arrest and gathered in the town and headed for the barracks. Just as the crowd arrived, some eighty RIC men poured out the front doors and launched themselves at the crowd, hitting left and right with their batons. All that night there were running battles around the town. It was a sure sign that the growing conflict was creating a divide that would prove irreparable.

By the time he had enrolled as an art student in the second half of the 1920s, however, O'Hickey had moved away from violence and sought to create his own future in art. His image – with that of Hayes – is now immortalised in Sean Keating's painting in a beautiful gallery in an independent city.

## Team Spirit

The Italian artist Salvatore Garau sold an invisible sculpture for €15,000 in 2022. This was twice the reserve price. The sculpture is entitled 'Io Sono' ('I am' in Italian).

Apparently, the fact that all the buyer received was a certificate of authentication that is signed and stamped by Garau does not seem to have raised any alarm bells.

As if to underline the sheer extent of his audacity, Garau is said to have set down instructions that the sculpture be displayed in an area five feet long by five feet wide, in a private home, unhindered by any obstruction.

Basically, he didn't want nothing to be obscured by anything or something.

A magnificent piece of reporting on the sale of the invisible statue in *Newsweek* included the following deadpan line: 'Because the piece does not exist, there are no special lighting or climate requirements.'

It is not clear either what the security arrangements are – but it cannot be easy to protect something that cannot be seen. In the same way that TV viewers of a certain age will remember the havoc wreaked by the Invisible Man, originally the creation of H.G. Wells, and a figure so prominent in popular culture that versions of the story continue to emerge on film, audio drama and comics.

According to Garau, however, his sculpture is not nothing; instead it is actually a 'vacuum', and its purpose is to activate a person's imagination. And as an engineer patiently explained, a 'vacuum is a space in which nothing affects any processes being carried on there'. And we all know how important processes are to sport …!

The €15,000 'Io Sono' is only the latest of Garau's pieces. As he said of another of his invisible sculptures (in the middle of Piazza della Scala in Milan): 'It is made of air and spirit.'

If you could own air and spirit – and if you could own a vacuum and use it to stimulate and inspire and activate every human's imagination – it could legitimately be claimed that

€15,000 would actually be an exceptionally cost-effective investment.

Teams that play with spirit, that seem to own the air, that are inspired and stimulated, that set about a game in a way that fills the imagination are exactly what sport demands. It is something that is sought by participants and spectators alike.

But how do you define these things? How do you measure spirit?

The modern insistence for reducing sport to a series of statistical categories is all pervasive. It is something that is now wrapped around every meaningful match in every significant sport.

Even many low-ranking teams have a small army of analysts who deliver real-time statistics into a dressing-room at half-time and at full-time. More detailed analysis is provided in the days that follow. These are later bounded together to offer the profile of a season, then of a run of seasons. There is a merit in that. If you can deal in facts, in hard evidence, it makes every decision easier, gives ballast to every piece of instruction and coaching. Every sport has technical things that can be improved through coaching: it's a hard, relentless, frustrating, repetitive grind to truly make advances. But technical advance without spirit carries only limited merit when the air gets thinner.

In the summer of 2022, the veteran Kerry player David Moran said that the team spirit within the Kerry senior football panel was unlike anything he had experienced during his fourteen seasons playing for the team: 'It's just a close-knit squad. Winning helps too. Fellas just seem to get on. I'm not sure exactly where the team spirit is coming from, but it's good so far.'

In saying he wasn't sure precisely where the team spirit was coming from, Moran got right to the heart of things. As well as being hard to define, spirit is extraordinarily elusive to create. Every team may yearn for it, but intentions are one thing and actuality another.

The modern history of sport is littered with examples of men who promise to have access to the secret to this alchemy. Even those who appear to have it – or who may once have had it, like José Mourinho – come unstuck in the end.

Spirit is often connected with the 'culture' of a team. But that doesn't really help much either when you seek to break it down into practicalities. It is a commonplace now to hear people talk about the 'culture' in a team or a club; it is not always clear they know what they are talking about. In respect of sport and preparing a team, it is said in a vague way that 'culture' is a word that can be clarified as 'how things are done'.

That feels a little simplistic. Back towards the end of the last millennium, Raymond Williams (Welsh academic, novelist and critic who made the study of culture his life's work) wrote that culture was 'one of the two or three most complicated words in the English language'.

There is one very basic thing to say about this pursuit of 'spirit' and 'culture'. You can always see it in a team – this is true in victory and defeat. Equally you can see it when it's not there. In fact, it is in the negative aspect that it most often reveals itself. A team without spirit rots in front of your eyes.

There is no real science to it: you seek and strain, try to do everything right, but still it doesn't work. In part, it is in this absence of logic that some (or even much) of the glory and agony of sport can be found, in the not knowing what else to do.

Perhaps it would be at this point that a county board might consider commissioning a sculpture from Salvatore Garau. In fairness, there have been men across the island who gave spent money on greater madnesses in the pursuit of a medal.

# 5 CHILDREN

Growing up in Offaly in the 1970s and 1980s, the local sports day was a huge part of every year. We got the full day off school, granted because the sports day in Durrow was tied to the ancient tradition of Pattern Days. In our case it meant celebrating, on every 9 June, the life of St Columba and the existence of a holy well and a high cross down at Durrow Abbey. That high cross – a remarkable monument now open to the public in a restored setting – was down a wonderful tree-lined avenue. We paraded there as angelic altar boys after mass, organised behind banners, all the time looking forward to the sports in the afternoon. For us children there were running races, jumping events, sack races, egg-and-spoon and a whole range of novelty events. There were buckets of sweets and flogs and chocolate. For adults, there was a wheel-of-fortune, and hurling and football matches. The tradition of Pattern Days remains in some corners of Ireland, but other traditions with nothing to do with religion also survive. In the far corner of north Offaly close to the Laois border is the small village of Cloneygowan. My granny lived there and a great event every year was (and remains) the Gooseberry Fair. Just as in Durrow, it was a big thing for people who left the area to come back on that day every year. That fair, too, had the same athletic events and novelty games of the Durrow Pattern Day. It also had brilliant tug-o'-war competitions – a feat of strength and teamwork for which Irishmen were famed and for which several won gold medals at the London Olympics of 1908.

There is something in the sound of children playing sport that is timeless. That is not to say that it is something that is inherently good, that it should be devoid of analysis, or that there is one particular type of sporting childhood that must be adhered to. In *Barbarian Days*, his recollections of his life as a surfer, William Finnegan recalled growing up on the west coast of America. He described the casual carnage of a pre-video games world, where there was routinely boxing in the streets and random acts of cruelty, such as urinating in someone else's mouth. Finnegan described this as the 'ambient, low-grade violence' of his childhood growing up in an Irish-American family in the middle decades of the twentieth century. He had no interest in 'the club thing, the organised sports side', but he found a vital teenage outlet in surfing. This was a sporting life shaped not just by personal taste, but by being brought up in proximity to Malibu Beach, 'the imperial centre' of the sport, at a time of the massive explosion of interest in surfing that continued until it entered the mainstream of popular culture. It was not that he found salvation in the sport, but it did give him something when he needed it. And although he could leave the sport to one side for a time, he could also return to it when he wished.

It is also in childhood that the intense dislike expressed by people for sport can ordinarily be found. Usually this is related to school experiences, particularly in schools where sport is forced onto students or is elevated to a platform that is weird in its obsessive veneration. Remembrance of the taunting, sneering derision of some of those who thrived at sport understandably framed how some who were either unable or uninterested viewed sport and everything that goes with it. Such hatred as was not cultivated on the school grounds could also find plentiful impetus at home. This is the case not just for those whose parents made the uninterested play sport, but also among those who liked sport and were good at it, but found themselves the vehicles for parents who sought to live their own thwarted dreams through their children.

## No Ordinary Sports Day

You hear them before you see them. It's something glorious: the high-pitched, joyous, unending scream of children at a sports day.

The sun is burning the sky and over in the stand there are kids up on the seats, jumping and yelling; along the railings others are straining out over the track, roaring support and clapping; and, a little further away, all around the lovely ampitheatre that is the Morton Stadium in Santry, there are groups of primary school children, their teachers and a speckle of parents.

An under-10 sprint is coming down the home straight and the girls are a microcosm of the modern ethnic composition of Dublin's classrooms. They are wearing the colours of their schools and they fly down the track to the sound of ever-louder cheers. It is scene that is repeated in race after race from 10am until the early afternoon – a triumph of organisation that is a tribute to those who give their time to make this day happen.

As these races are run, above the bottom turn of the track a small group of girls are rolling down a grassy bank and laughing their heads off – and then doing it over and over again. About thirty other girls are turning cartwheels, almost in unison. Two boys are wrestling each other beneath the flagpoles, and over a bit further another boy seems to be trying to push a straw up his friend's nose. This ends in another wrestling match. Further along again, a gang of twenty or so boys are just hanging out, the hippest eight-year-olds ever to chill in this neighbourhood.

For all the talk about how different life now is for children, there is also much that is essentially the same. The fun of a sports day is something that is familiar to all, something that is a shared experience across generations, something recognisable from everybody's past.

This is no ordinary sports day, however: it's the Dublin Schools' Athletics Finals; to be here is a magical experience. There are hundreds of children entered to run. Between races they roam around Morton Stadium like the great herds of the Savannah, as if they have wandered in from one of David Attenborough's nature films.

It is a wonderful antidote: there's an awful lot to be cynical about in the modern world of athletics. The travesty that is the Olympic Games routinely dishonours the meaning of athletics. The brilliance, commitment and integrity of honest athletes end up being tarnished by the drug cheats and dopers of all hues who mean that it is now impossible to entirely believe in anyone who wins. That is an awful thing for those who are clean, but it is the inevitable legacy of the crooks who have gone before them and of the administrators who have singularly failed their sports.

In essence, to believe that athletics at the Olympic Games will be clean of drug winners is to believe that the earth is shaped like one big pancake. If the sport of athletics can be considered as a spectrum, the Olympics track and field championships lie debased at one end, and what is happening at Santry sits at the opposite extreme entirely.

As the hours roll on, the tannoy system calls boys and girls to races and calls out, also, the winners of those races. It is a reminder, of course, that this is a day that is laced with disappointment for some. It is a hard thing to be the fastest child in your school, the fastest child on your street, even the fastest child you know. But then you meet somebody who's faster and they beat you in front of a crowd. The bitter tears of defeat flow freely beside the track at Santry: nothing anyone says can change the fact of loss or change the cruelty of that feeling. Time – and the pockmarks of the inevitable defeats still to come – will put the defeat of this day in context, for better or for worse. Today is a hard day to lose, if you expect – and are expected – to win.

Then there are those that do win – children so naturally athletic that the elegance of their movement is beyond grace. Or their raw power, even at this early age, is so overwhelming that it is undeniable. When power and elegance run together, it is thrilling to watch, regardless of the age of the athlete. It is an entirely natural thing to wonder if one of these runners will one day compete in a bigger stadium and on a bigger stage. Did someone look at Sonia running at a school sports or across a park or down the road and see in her stride the making of a world champion and an Olympic medallist?

But just as it is natural to ask that question, it is only right to ask also whether you would wish that on them. The sacrifices, the compromises, the sheer obsession that is needed to rise to the top can strip a life of balance and create hazards that are not always overcome. It can be done, of course. Travelling the spectrum from school sports to Olympic Games reveals much about character and resilience. It is also an opportunity to be true to yourself and your sport.

At the core of it all is a love of running.

This is a love that is evident all morning at Santry, where an eleven-year-old boy has just brought home the baton in first place in the 400m relay race. He is so ecstatic in the moment that he leaps in the air and screams in joy. All around people are cheering and clapping, and his teammates mob him. It is easy to lose yourself in his moment – the thrill of winning, the thrill of running, the promise of a future that stretches out beyond a field in Santry into a blue sky.

## A Free Kick

The fading light of a Saturday afternoon in the back field at Westmanstown GAA Club in west Dublin.

The under-14 girls Féile football semi-final between Skerries Harps and St Oliver Plunketts-Eoghan Ruadh is in a sudden-death shootout. The girls have finished level after extra-time – a great game that flew up and down the field from start to finish, as two excellent, well-matched teams tore into each other.

Now, sudden-death free kicks from the 20m line have been going on for more than a quarter of an hour. The teams are deadlocked after eleven kicks apiece – scores and misses stepping perfectly beside each other. A Plunketts player – we'll call her Cáit – is next up. Like many of the girls on both teams, she is destroyed with tension. She has to be coaxed to take the kick. It's a bit like the way stable-hands try to push a deeply reluctant horse into the stalls before a race.

Up she goes, eventually, in a slow march and takes the ball from the referee. She stands just behind the 20m line and it's quiet. She swings her right foot. The ball arcs beautifully between the posts. She has never kicked a ball like this before – in fact, she almost never scores. Normally, she runs and chases and tackles and wins breaks and passes the ball on to others – but doesn't score or even shoot.

But now this – a winning point. For the team coach – her father – there is, in that moment, pure, unrestrained joy. A few tears may have been shed – or maybe a small bucket of them.

The best sporting moment of the decade – this one and every other.

# 6 HEROES

Through media – first in newspapers and magazines, and then on radio – the creation of heroes played a fundamental part in shaping the modern sporting world. This was subsequently magnified with the mass televising of sporting events. The 2011 film *Senna*, directed by Asif Kapadia, is the ultimate example of the manner in which the camera reframes the life of the modern sporting hero. There were cameras everywhere in the professional life of the Brazilian racing driver Ayrton Senna as he passed from boyhood to global sporting star, multiple angles which bring the viewer into Senna's world – even into his helmet – as he becomes a multiple world champion. Those cameras also recorded his death and afterlife. The footage of the brutal crash which took Senna's life at the San Marino Grand Prix at Imola in 1994 is followed in the film by extraordinary scenes as 'the whole of Brazil is seen weeping along with his intimates'. In his review of the film, Michael Wood wrote: 'There is no mistaking what has happened for these grieving crowds: a god has died.'

The story of Senna is an amplified version of the one lived by stars in many sports. Television brought national and then international recognition to sportspeople whose fame would have been much more local in any previous era. But it has also, in many instances, served to limit the duration of much of that fame. There are sporting heroes such as Senna who transcend time and place, but they are relatively few. While the media (now including social media and other internet-based technologies) is instrumental in polishing the legend that affords a person greatness, the very nature of this media – and of the protean world of sport – ensures that the arena constantly demands new glories. In this churn, only a select few truly survive beyond the immediacy of their triumphs. Most fade away into a nostalgia of yellowing newsprint, of sepia photographs, of old footage that sits out of shape and in blurred focus on modern screens. Their sporting deeds are a matter of record, but they retreat in the public mind, shouldered to the margins by new stars, who themselves ultimately will follow the same path into the void of obscurity.

## Christy Ring

Christy Ring is one of the select few names in the history of Irish sport who truly transcends his own era. It is impossible to discuss the greatest ever hurlers without Ring being central to the conversation. Even those judges who do not agree that Christy Ring was the greatest hurler of all time must account for him in their reckoning.

This is a gloriously inexact science. The endless unseen incidents in every sporting event can make a mockery of any framework which pretends to rank greatness. When these events are placed one after the next into the context of sporting lives, the challenge of assessing the relative merits of individual careers becomes all the more difficult.

So what are the measures of greatness that define a sporting life? The recorded successes of a sportsperson obviously matter in any reckoning with greatness. This is particularly true of individual sports; there is a dent in the legend of any man or woman who does not achieve the ultimate accolade in their sport. That dent is not necessarily a defining one, but it must be considered. The heroic loss should not be dismissed; a truly outstanding sporting career can play out in defeat in the face of opposition which turns out to be insurmountable. Normally, though, success in sport – and, by extension, the inevitable failure of others – is essential to acclamations of greatness.

This is more complicated in team sports where rooting greatness in a medal collection, or in the number of caps won, or in the length of time played at the highest level, is a much more limiting practice. Did a player make a team look great, or did the team make a player look great? How do you parse the collective greatness of a team? Does that greatness have to be measured on an international scale, as against one that is local or national?

There is no arguing with Christy Ring's haul of medals – eight All-Ireland medals (three as captain), nine Munster championship medals, four National Hurling Leagues, and eighteen Railway Cup winner's medals. What matters, also, is the context of victory. The capacity of players to bend a game to their will, to forge a victory when all appeared lost, or at least uncertain, is an essential element. This matter of context is always important. A key measure of sporting greatness lies not just in the sporting act itself, but in the timing of that act.

The list of Ring's key interventions are long, but here are just two – game-breaking scores against a brilliant Limerick team in the 1944 Munster final and against Kilkenny in the 1946 All-Ireland final.

In the making of a sporting hero, how you win can also be important. Most often this is a matter of aesthetics. The grace and skill of a brilliant sports person is singularly captivating. In a lovely biography of Ring, published in the *Dictionary of Irish Biography*, John A. Murphy writes that he 'made the game of hurling a living art form'.

Bob Bishop (chief Northern Ireland scout for Manchester United), was so enchanted by a first sighting of George Best on a Belfast soccer field that he telegrammed Matt Busby, United's manager, with words that have entered mythology: 'I think I have found a genius.' But skill is only one aspect of the aesthetic; power, courage, persistence, resilience, passion and much else are also relevant. For example, there were more skilful players than Nicky Rackard but he was 'powerfully built', 'tall and burly', and he 'fearlessly challenged defenders with his exceptional strength'. He could hurl, but he was also ferocious; the same was said of Ring.

In all of this, there must be fear of hagiography. In his book *Over the Bar*, Breandán Ó hEithir – the writer and broadcaster from the Aran Islands – spoke of how he got to know Christy Ring while making a film of the skills of hurling with him in the 1960s. The film is a beautiful piece of work. Ó hEithir was a brave writer who was willing to put in print unpopular things. Crucially, he did not believe in idolatry and he offered a rounded portrait of Ring: 'While I found his dedication to hurling admirable, his skills formidable and his company most congenial, I must confess that I found his fierce competitiveness repellent and somewhat frightening. It did not apply to hurling only. Winning in any sport he took up was of the utmost importance to him. This attitude is beyond my own comprehension and seems to enter the realm of fanaticism.'

Deciding where the line of acceptability in all of this is often related to the greatest intangible of all – how a sports person makes you feel. This is something that draws on dash and style and flair, and on unquenchable courage. Nobody who saw Christy Ring play doubted his bravery or his spirit.

But Ring was also beloved because – in his daily life – he walked among those who revered him; this hero is a man who spent much of his days in the cab of a lorry.

In all of this, the subjective is everywhere. But in the making of an ordered list of heroes, who gets to decide the relative merits of one medal collection over another? Who says it is one particular individual in a particular team sport who is the catalyst for victory? Who judges the beauty of one person's sporting prowess as being superior to another? How do you define courage? What can be more personal than a dream?

It is in this subjectivity that people find heroes. There is nothing new in the idea that sporting ability is a way to demonstrate and explain heroism. This is something that reaches back across history and into myth.

In Standish O'Grady's *Cuculain: An Epic* (1882), Cú

Chulainn was recast as a hero for the 1880s, his deeds as a hurler recreated for a new generation: when he played a match 'the clash of the metal hurles [*sic*] resounded in the evening air' and those who watch were awed into silence. Only the very best hurlers attempted to compete with him as he rushed backwards and forwards 'urging the ball in any direction that he pleased, as if in mockery'.

Ring stands in this tradition. As John A. Murphy wrote: 'Ring's iconic place in Cork tradition is reflected in photographic and verse displays in private and public houses. Partly because of the antiquity of the game, he has the folk status of a pre-historic hurling gaiscíoch (warrior, champion), typified by the many legendary occasions when, in heroic Cú Chulainn style, he would snatch victory in the face of defeat.'

## Eddie Heron

Friday, 23 August 1968.

Eddie Heron stands on the board three metres above the Blackrock Baths. It is a warm Friday night in Dublin and a big crowd have gathered to watch the Irish national diving championships. Waiting for Eddie to dive is the reigning champion George Matulevicze of the Ulster Swimming Club, who has already won the one-metre springboard championship earlier in the day. Also waiting is the brilliant Kevin Carter of Bangor Swimming Club, himself a former winner of the championship on six occasions.

It is Eddie who the crowd are here to see, however. He has been diving off the boards at Blackrock Baths all his life and is a member of the Sandycove Swimming Club who had originated at nearby Forty-Foot, but now use Blackrock Baths as their home base.

He is their darling, the greatest of them all.

Two things now happen just as they have always happened when Eddie Heron jumps from a springboard into a pool to the cheers of the crowd: he dives beautifully, hitting the water with glorious precision – and he wins. Across ten dives Eddie scores a total of 108.89 points. This puts him more than twenty points ahead of Matulevicze who finishes second with 88.21 points and Carter who come third with 83.17 points.

Eddie Heron is Irish 3-metre springboard champion. Again.

But this is different. It is 1968 and he is fifty-seven years of age. And he has not competed in the Irish championships for some eighteen years. Eddie had retired from competing in the Irish championships as far back as 1950. By then he had won thirty-four Irish national senior titles. His first year competing at senior level had been as long ago as 1924 when he came third in the Tailteann Games (to Olympic Gold medalist Dick Eve and Irish champion Charlie Batt). He was just thirteen at the time – later in that year of 1924 he had won the first of his Leinster senior high diving titles and he dominated that competition year after year over the next three decades.

There were high points to Eddie's dominance. In 1933 he became the only Irish man to win the British Open high-diving championship – either side of that victory he was placed second and deemed unlucky not to have won. But, best of all, his diving exhibitions as he travelled around Ireland drew thousands of people to see him display his extraordinary talent. Watching Eddie run through his repertoire of dives was something rare and gorgeous.

There was a sadness, too. In 1936, he would have been a serious contender for Olympic gold but a dispute over partition ensured that Ireland did not send a team to the Berlin Games. By the time he did finally get to compete at an Olympic Games – London in 1948 – he was no longer at his best and did not feature in the medals. Two years later in 1950 he slipped into retirement – the greatest diver the country had ever seen. A man so brilliant that in 1976 he became the only water-sports person to be elected to the Texaco Sports Stars Hall of Fame.

So why did Eddie Heron come out of retirement in 1968 at the age of fifty-seven?

The first and practical answer is that his club – Sandycove Swimming Club – pressed him to do so. They could find no diver to represent the club so they pushed Eddie to compete. Eventually he agreed. But there is something else that matters here: Heron was in a position to agree to dive because he had never stopped diving in the first place.

After he finished formally competing, he continued to swim in the sea at Sandycove and he continued to dive at Blackrock Baths. When he was well into his sixties – and even into his seventies – large crowds continued to gather to watch him dive.

Memoirs of people who grew up in Blackrock recall seeing Heron's extraordinary athleticism as he climbed the steps again and again to jump from the highest board. They recall seeing him twist and jackknife in the air, straighten and then shoot into the water.

There was obviously something in Eddie that loved the applause of the crowd, loved performing and loved competing, but most of all must have been the love of diving itself. This was something that had come to him from his father, a butcher who had originally come from Co. Carlow and who had been a passionate diver and gymnast.

Initially living in a small terraced house, just off the North Circular Road in Dublin, Eddie had been shown how to dive by his father from the age of four. Later, Eddie moved to Blackrock and worked as a bookie in the village. In retirement he continued to live in the area, becoming one of those figures that transcends the generations. On his death in 1985 he was buried in Shanganagh Cemetery and it was as part of a series of articles written by Gabriel Conroy in a local magazine called *Scan* that his story was retold.

The Blackrock Baths are now gone, but a plaque near the location is dedicated to Eddie and an annual race in his honour is organised every year by Sandycove Swimming Club from Dun Laoghaire to Blackrock. None of these matter to Eddie now, of course. Neither could he take his medals with him. Winning mattered, obviously, but what really matters is that he lived a life in sport. The meaning of the memorials to his name lies in their significance to those who swim and dive for competition and for pleasure. They honour the man, but also honour a sport that lives towards the margins of Irish sporting life and is no less beloved of its adherents than any other.

## Mabel Cahill

Mabel Cahill could not be found.

Back in the 1890s, she won five US Open tennis championships. But then Mabel Cahill fell off the cliff of history.

The speculation was that she had left America for England later in the 1890s. There were whispers that she had been seen attending the Wimbledon championships some time shortly after 1900.

But there was nothing concrete, nothing more than half-suggestions – and there was certainly no evidence that she had come back to her homeplace of Ballyragget in Co. Kilkenny.

Occasional informal inquiries brought no news and so, in 1936, Harry Maunsell drafted a note to send to the newspapers. He was the secretary of the Irish Lawn Tennis Association and that association wished to honour the fact that in 1891 and 1892, Mabel Cahill had won two singles, two women's doubles and two mixed doubles championships at the US Open.

A gold medallion was to be struck in her honour – Cahill was, after all, the most successful tennis player that Ireland had ever produced.

The note to the press circulated by Maunsell read: 'Will Miss Mabel E. Cahill, the winner of the Women's United States Singles Championship in 1891 and 1892, or her representatives, kindly communicate with the hon. Sec. of the ILTA, 91 Merrion Square, Dublin, relative to a gold medallion which can be claimed on her behalf.'

Nothing happened.

Four decades later, in 1976, Mabel Cahill was inducted into the Tennis Hall of Fame at Rhode Island. The Hall of Fame was opened in 1955 and Cahill was one of the first non-Americans to enter into it. But even then, there was no story of her life, no news of what had become of her.

The search for Mabel Cahill continued in the new millennium. In 2006 Tom Higgins produced a monumental three-volume history of tennis in Ireland which extended across some 1,774 pages. The scale of the research was breathtaking on every conceivable aspect of tennis, but the author was forced to write of Cahill: 'This lady has proved a bit of a mystery.'

This was gorgeous understatement. But it is something that can no longer be said.

Mabel Cahill has been reclaimed for history by Mark Ryan, who published his work on the tennisforum.com website. It is a masterpiece of biographical research – and a genuinely tragic tale.

She was born in 1863, the twelfth eldest of thirteen children of Michael Cahill (a barrister and land agent) and Margaret Magan. The family lived at Ballyconra house in the small Kilkenny town of Ballyragget.

Although both her parents died before she finished school, Mabel Cahill (along with several of her siblings) were active in the social life of Co. Kilkenny in the 1880s. That social life – for the elite of the county of which Mabel could have been considered part – included lawn tennis parties and tournaments.

The craze for lawn tennis had swept through Ireland, just as it had England – in the late 1870s and early 1880s. Little was more fashionable than garden parties that included tennis tournaments. Major events such as the national tennis championships in Fitzwilliam Square in Dublin were essential events on the social calendar of high society.

In 1886 Cahill played in those championships, before emigrating to America in the late 1880s. She lived in Manhattan – alongside Central Park – and began playing tennis in the new courts built in that park. Then, as she established herself in the city where one of her brothers also now lived, she became a member of the New York Tennis Club in 1890.

Later that summer she travelled across to Philadelphia and was the only non-American of the eight women to compete for the singles championship. She lost to Ellen Roosevelt, the eventual winner of the competition.

The following year she returned and exacted revenge. She defeated both Grace and Ellen Roosevelt to claim the honours. The final victory over Ellen Roosevelt was 6–4, 6–1, 4–6, 6–3 in a best of five sets match.

She then added the women's doubles championship to her singles success – and duly came back in 1892 to repeat this double. To extend her record, she also added the mixed doubles championship, becoming the first man or woman to record a treble at a major championship.

Mabel Cahill was now a sporting star and a syndicated article about her appeared in the American press. The article described her as 'a petite, attractive brunette, with short black hair, and the brightest of grey eyes, full of life and spirits. Although a champion of America, she is a daughter of Erin.'

Mabel Cahill explained her success: 'On coming here I played at first in the park, being a stranger among tennis players generally. On becoming better acquainted, I was asked to join the New York Tennis Club, where I have played ever since. I have improved very much since coming here, which is due largely to playing against men, the advantages of such practice being far superior to playing with even the best lady players.'

Indeed, newspaper references from the era refer to Cahill's 'manliness' and pay tribute to the ferocity of her groundstrokes and her energy around the court. It was a hugely successful approach. As the syndicated article went on to mention: 'Miss Cahill was too modest to admit that she defeats, with few exceptions, her male opponents. The principal feature of Miss Cahill's playing is her activity. On the tennis court she seems to be everywhere at once and her opponents find it difficult to place a ball out of her reach. Those who have never seen her play can form no idea of the dash and spirit she puts into her game.'

The whole story ended on an upswing: 'Miss Cahill has only kind things to say of American and Americans. She likes New York so well it will probably be her permanent home.'

By then, Cahill was also working to forge a career as a writer. She published a novel in New York in 1891, entitled *Her playthings, men*. It was not a success. She tried shorter stories – 'Carved in Marble' and 'Purple Sparkling' – but they too died a death. Her fiction was essentially an attempt to write of the life of single women in a modern city but her style was plodding, her characters unlikeable and the capacity to sustain a story over an extended span was not exactly evident.

Struggling with fiction, she moved to try a sort of journalism and in June and July 1893 she contributed two articles to the *Ladies' Home Journal*, under the titles, respectively, of 'The art of playing good tennis' and 'Arranging a tennis tournament'. These, too, were mediocre in quality.

Then the record of her writing dwindles and disappears.

Presumably struggling to live in New York, Mabel Cahill headed to London in 1897. She was by then thirty-four and was most likely ill, and possibly destitute. Either ways she was admitted to the Liverpool Road Workhouse in April 1897.

Nonetheless, she began to earn money in the city, writing articles for magazines and performing on stage in music halls where she sang and acted in variety performances.

She was not one to tangle with. In 1899 she represented herself as she sued Sydney Vecker of the Royal Muncaster Theatre in Bootle for £5 she claimed was owed to her. Vecker argued that Cahill was essentially working for free on a trial basis until he decided whether she was good enough or not. The judge decided in favour of Cahill and awarded her £5 plus costs.

It was one of her last victories. The challenges in piecing back together a life are revealed in that for the next five years it is unclear what Mabel Cahill did. Then, in late 1904 or in early 1905 she was admitted to a workhouse in the Lancashire town of Ormskirk. She may have been living in the area to work in the great seaside music halls of nearby Blackpool and Southport.

Her health was in precipitative decline – she was run through with TB. On 2 February 1905, Mabel Cahill died in the Union Workhouse in Ormskirk. Three days later she was buried in a pauper's grave in the graveyard of the Church of Saint Peter and Saint Paul.

This was the most bleak of endings to a life that had begun with birth into relative wealth and status and had reached the heights of entry into the upper echelons of American society.

The cruelty of the descent was rendered all the more poignant by the subsequent disappearance from history. Mark Ryan deserves great credit for his labours to remake the life and times of Ireland's most successful ever tennis player – a woman whose story, both in its heights and its depths, is deeply human and a sharp reminder of the vagaries of the world.

If nothing else, Mabel Cahill has now been found.

## Martin Sheridan

At Swinford railway station on Friday, 31 July 1908, a young Irish emigrant jumped down onto the platform carrying a case with his clothes in it. He was back in Mayo and intent on travelling to his father's farm outside the nearby village of Bohola. His name was Martin Sheridan – he had emigrated at the age of eighteen to America and now, nine years later, he worked for the New York police. This was no typical emigrant journey home, however. When the train carrying Sheridan pulled into the town, the Swinford Band began playing 'See The Conquering Hero Comes' – and all the approach roads to the train station were thronged with people.

Martin Sheridan wanted to slip quietly home to see his family – but that wasn't easy when you have just won two gold medals in discus throwing and one long jump bronze at an Olympic Games. Those medals – won at the London Olympics – proved the crowning glory of Sheridan's career. By the time he retired from athletics he had won five gold, three silver and one bronze medal at Olympic Games. He had also created sixteen world records in various track and field disciplines, as well as winning multiple US championships.

Now, though, his great challenge would be to make it through Swinford. He had told nobody that he was coming home, but news of his presence on the train had been wired from Dublin to Swinford. The news then spread like a prairie fire across that town – and out into the countryside.

A public meeting, a banquet in the Commercial Hotel, and a reception were immediately organised. Photographs were taken of him holding the discus at various places, including at the back of Lambe's pub. And, of course, he had to make a speech. That speech is still wonderful to read. It was laced with modesty and humour and even politics. The fact that Ireland was not an independent country, he said, was an injustice which had to end. There was also the bitter regret that he had emigrated because there was no future before him in Ireland – and that there seemed to be no future for any lad his age.

Mostly, though, his words were a celebration of pride in coming from a rural area in Co. Mayo and conquering the world. 'I am once more with my own,' he said, 'and I don't think there are twenty people in this room who are not related to me in some way or other. In many a hard-fought contest, when only inches lay between me and the prize, I have often thought of you, and these thoughts never failed to make me gird my energies and drive my Swinford blood coursing madly through my veins in my efforts to achieve victory.'

The wild applause in Swinford was nothing compared to the reception in Bohola, where a magnificent open-air meeting was staged. His parents – Joe and Kitty – were there to hear Martin feted by, among others, the schoolteacher who had taught him his ABCs.

The rest of August 1908 was a whirl. He did get moments of relaxation around home – he shot rabbits and wild ducks, and swam regularly in the River Moy, but there was no long-term escape from his new celebrity.

Everywhere that Martin Sheridan went, he was met by huge crowds. The trains he took were stopped at every station to allow local people meet him and sing to him. In Dublin he was carried shoulder high from Broadstone train station to the Lord Mayor's carriage and on to a reception at the Gresham Hotel.

He went down to Dungarvan in Co. Waterford to meet another outstanding Irish athlete from those years: Tom Kiely from Tipperary. Kiely had won an Olympic medal as All-Round Champion (a sort of forerunner of the modern decathlon) in St Louis in 1904. He returned to America in 1906 and won the All-Round World Championship in 1906. He had done so without defeating Sheridan, who won the title in 1905, 1907 and 1909, but was injured in 1906 and could not compete against Kiely. Kiely was by 1908 well into his thirties and was a ferocious competitor. He and Sheridan competed against each other across five events in Dungarvan. The contest was a brilliant one which enthralled the crowd for an afternoon, before ending in a draw. The men shook hands and promised to resolve the battle for superiority on another day. Later in August, Martin Sheridan also competed at a sports day in Dundalk and, using the discus he had won with in London, broke the world record.

His final sporting activity in Ireland came a few weeks later when he competed back in Mayo in the Ballina Sports. So great was the crush at the gate that the men who were attempting to collect the entrance fee simply abandoned their posts. As one observer noted: 'One might as well seek to keep the tide out with a proverbial fork.' Tom Kiely had travelled up from Dungarvan, but was unable to compete against Sheridan due to a back injury. The highpoint of the sports was a pole-vaulting exhibition which Sheridan gave to thunderous applause.

Three days later, on 8 September 1908, hundreds of people returned to Swinford train station to see Martin Sheridan off from his hometown. He headed to Queenstown (now Cobh) in Co. Cork and took a Cunard Line ferry to New York where he returned to work in the police department. He retired from athletics in 1911 at the age of thirty, but progressed through the police ranks, becoming a detective and serving as special bodyguard to the Governor of New York.

On Saturday, 23 March 1918, a group of his friends organised a surprise party for him to celebrate his thirty-seventh birthday. The party never happened. Sheridan had been admitted to hospital the previous day, suffering from pneumonia. He rallied and slipped and rallied again – until, five days later, his condition deteriorated rapidly and he died on 27 March 1918.

A huge crowd attended his funeral – the men he worked with and played with wept openly on the street. In the months and years that followed, medals and cups were named in his honour, monuments were erected in America and in Ireland, and his memory remained alive in song and verse. He was – as the inscription on his gravestone reads –

An Intrepid American,
An ardent lover of his motherland;
A Peerless athlete;
Devoted to the institutions of his country
And to the ideals and aspirations of his race.

# 7 REBELLION

The most awkward thing about history is its endless capacity to undermine belief. There is a basic human desire for clarity of thought, for things to be boxed up neatly. But history doesn't permit that. The complexities, nuances, even the contradictions of how people have thought and behaved in Ireland are apparent in its sports. But this sits at odds with the crude caricatures beloved of propagandists who want to indulge in cartoon history allowing stereotypes and gross distortions to prosper as inherited truths. It is true that it is possible to pick selectively from the history of Ireland's major sporting organisations and create a very particular image of that organisation. This is especially true when the historical divide is presented as being between 'native games' and 'foreign games'.

How did this happen? How was it that games organised according to different – but similar – rules should have emerged as badges of national identity, used at will as rhetorical weapons? The timing of the nineteenth-century revolution in play was crucial; the British Empire was expanding its wealth and power at precisely the moment the modern sporting world was forged. The fact that Ireland was by then part of the United Kingdom of Great Britain and Ireland helped ensure that nowhere were the games of empire more rapidly and more fully adopted. In short, in the late nineteenth and early twentieth centuries, British imperial culture flourished in Ireland. Many Irish nationalists were entirely comfortable with the sports of empire; they chose to play as they wished regardless of any association with Britishness; they did not consider their Irishness in any way compromised by their sporting affiliations.

Others, though, afloat on ideas of cultural nationalism, saw in sport the possibilities of furthering the project of national liberation. In practical terms, this resulted in the establishment of a uniquely Irish sporting institution: the Gaelic Athletic Association. This institution promoted games described as 'Irish native games' and bathed them in ideas of Irishness. What ensued was a struggle for sporting supremacy between rival sporting organisations in the social, cultural and political context of a divided island.

But those who played sport did not necessarily belong to the tribe they were said to belong to by virtue of their sporting choice. Rather, sport in Ireland developed as a shared culture across time and place. Disentangling the motives and the meaning of the decisions that people made in their sporting choices is fraught with difficulty. Indeed, what is most obvious in the modern era is the manner in which the boundaries between sporting organisations and their relationships with people on the island were anything but monolithic. The shadow cast by this history on Irish sport remains a real one – it remains bound up in debates about Irishness and national identity. From sporting organisations to political entities and from sports people to entrepreneurial officials, the history of Irish sport has been soaked in invention. Too often there is no attempt at contextualisation. This matters, most of all, because it symbolises something which extends far beyond sport, something that is revealed every day in the modern world: the sense that it is somehow acceptable to manipulate facts, to disregard unhelpful evidence, to present as truth something that is patently false, to lie and lie again.

But even if there was no invention, no attempt to deceive or to burnish, history creates challenges to those who wish the past to fall into neat lines. This was made plain during the decade of revolution in Ireland, 1912–23, when the politics of national identity gripped ever more tightly on sport. The introduction to the House of Commons in April 1912 of a bill giving Home Rule to Ireland was followed by two years of escalating tension and, ultimately, the militarisation of large sections of the civilian population. Determined to resist the introduction of Home Rule, unionists formed the Ulster Volunteers and pledged never to accept the rule of Dublin. Nationalists responded with the establishment of their own Irish Volunteers. This loosed a series of events which led ultimately to the establishment of the Irish Free State on a partitioned island in 1922. These events included a Rising in Dublin against the backdrop of world war, a subsequent War of Independence fought between an Irish Republican Army (IRA) and British forces between 1919 and 1921, and then a civil war where members of the IRA fought each other in 1922 and 1923. Sport was entangled in every aspect of this decade, but not in narrow, neatly separated stripes of green and orange.

As if to remind us of how uncompliant the past is with the political demands of the present, there is a letter in the National Library of Ireland written by Alec Wilson to Alice Stopford Green, the historian and nationalist, written in June 1914, just as tensions in Ireland had dramatically worsened and civil war appeared imminent. Wilson, a landholder in Co. Down, noted that local members of the Ulster Volunteers and the Irish Volunteers had agreed to share the cost of building a rifle range on his lands. More than that, both forces had marched home together after attending an illegal cockfight in Co. Cavan. The shared interest in a gamble on bloodletting conquered all divides.

## Rugby and War

Easter Saturday, 1916.

A huge crowd has gathered at Lansdowne Road for a match between Ulster and Leinster. This is no normal game, however. The Great War is continuing to produce slaughter on an industrial scale and the normal rugby calendar has been suspended. In its place is a series of charity matches to raise money for injured soldiers, or the dependants of dead ones. Or to send things to the Western Front to make the lives of soldiers in the trenches more bearable.

The match in Lansdowne Road is billed as a 'Crock's Match' – veteran players line out to represent Ulster and Leinster. A huge crowd turn out to see 'the best game we have seen since the war broke out'. Among the players are nineteen former Irish internationals, some of whom played for Ireland back in the nineteenth century. Others are soldiers who are actually home for Easter, on leave from service in the British Army, and they include at least one serving major.

The players gather together and pose for a photograph before the game – just as teams always do – in front of the main stand. Behind the moustaches and the slicked hair and the starched shirts, there is an obvious pride in the prospect of once more representing their province at Lansdowne Road. The men are ageing, yet they mostly carry it well – filling their jerseys, but not overfilling them.

Over to the extreme right of the photograph sits Frank Browning. Browning is wearing a buttoned-up white shirt and a tie and a solid moustache and a mid-parting in his hair that is under a little bit of pressure. This is the last rugby match that Frank Browning will ever organise: two days later – on Easter Monday – he will be shot dead by members of the Irish Volunteers on a street just around the corner from Lansdowne Road.

How did this happen?

In the weeks after the Great War began, the Irish Rugby Football Union Volunteer Corps had been founded by Frank Browning. He had called on the players and officials of Dublin's rugby clubs 'to do their bit' and to join the war effort (just as the leader of Irish nationalism, John Redmond, also did). This corps mirrored similar sporting battalions in Britain where sporting clubs enlisted almost *en bloc*. Ultimately, more than 300 men joined the Irish Rugby Football Union Volunteer Corps, formally constituted as 'D' Company of the 7th Royal Dublin Fusiliers.

Men who were deemed too old to fight in the regular army formed a home battalion and – dressed in green uniforms – took on duties in support of the regular British army in Dublin. This battalion – led by Browning – were returning to Dublin from routine manoeuvres in Wicklow on Easter Monday 1916 when they headed straight into the rebellion which had begun in their absence. Led by Patrick Pearse and Tom Clarke, a small group of Irish nationalists were determined to use the war to assert Irish independence and, joined by members of James Connolly's Irish Citizen Army, had secretly planned for rebellion. Close to Beggars Bush Barracks, Frank Browning and six other members of his corps were shot dead in an ambush by rebels who were guarding the entry routes to the city.

The great certainty of war is death. A man who two days previously stood to get his photograph taken with a rugby team lay dying in a pool of blood.

The year 1916 brought war and death on a scale that was unprecedented in Ireland. The roll-call of the dead, the dying and the injured mounted month after month, as the Great War lurched disastrously onwards. The scale of that war – and the sense that no end to it was in sight – had presented both the backdrop and the opportunity for another war. This second war – known to history as the Easter Rising – transformed the city of Dublin during Easter 1916 into a battleground of death and destruction, and ultimately transformed the politics of Ireland.

As both these wars recede into history there is a tendency to look at them increasingly in the abstract, as things that are remote from modern life. This tendency draws people to regard them as being as distant in their own way as the French Revolution or the Napoleonic Wars. They become, in this respect, understood by counting the numbers of those who fought and died, or in the way they redrew maps, nationally and internationally. Or in one-dimensional heroic tributes to 'patriotism' (or equally one-dimensional condemnation of such 'patriotism'), often paid by those seeking to make modern political capital by rattling the bones of the dead for their own ends.

But the real meaning of these wars lies in the individual stories of the people who were lost, and the people who were left behind. It is here that the true horror of both wars reveal themselves. In the course of the Great War at least fourteen Irish rugby internationals died, while others were permanently disabled. Many more club rugby players were also killed. These included, to give just one example from 1916, the Shannon junior rugby player Timothy Carroll who was killed in France. Numerous other rugby players also died in 1916, including many who fought in the Battle of the Somme. Whether they were unionist or nationalist in their allegiances mattered nothing in the churn of blood and flesh of northern France.

The Somme is a battle which has passed into memory as human tragedy on a grand scale. After the initial German advance into France had been halted in 1914, there was deadlock. Trenches were built along 450 miles of the Western Front which stretched from Belgium, through France and into the Swiss Alps. On 1 July 1916, the Allied forces sought to break the deadlock and launched a major offensive along a 40km front at the River Somme.

The offensive was confronted by strong German fortifications and the ensuing battle was devastating. The first day of the Battle of the Somme was the worst day in British military history. Some 20,000 men were killed and among the dead were thousands of Irishmen, mostly serving with the 36th (Ulster) Division. During the first two days of battle alone, the 36th (Ulster) Division – Carson's Men – lost 5,500 out of 15,000 men to death or injury at Thiepval.

The Somme offensive continued through the summer and autumn, and in September, the 16th (Irish) Division joined the action as they fought in battle at Guillemont and Ginchy. Again, there were heavy losses and amongst those who fell was Tom Kettle, the former nationalist MP and university professor.

The Battle of the Somme lasted until 18 November 1916 and resulted in the allies advancing five miles. By then, the bloodiest battle in world history had brought more than a million casualties – 420,000 from the British army, 195,000 French and 650,000 Germans. The bodies of many of those who died were never found.

From the streets of Dublin to the fields of France, the brutal impact of war was apparent for all to see in 1916. The abstract notion of 'blood sacrifice' – in the service of empire or of nation – was made real in old team photographs that now contained names and faces of rugby players and officials who were no longer alive.

When rugby began again to be played across Ireland in the aftermath of the Great War, the scars of war were all too apparent in the memory of those who were no longer present in clubhouses and dressing-rooms. This is, when it comes down to it, the cruel truth of the wars fought in 1916.

## Christmas, 1916

Christmas week means there's money to be made. The world is at war and the centre of Dublin lies in ruins from the rebellion at Easter, but the press of commerce is insistent.

Nolans in Tralee are selling scooters and roller skates and footballs.

Turkeys killed and ready to be killed are being sent on the boat to England. Before the war, the French had this market tied up – but not now, not with the blood that has flowed at the Somme and at Verdun. This year it is Irish turkeys that will sit proud and plump on English tables.

The mailboat is busy now and getting busier every day. Parcels are being sent to England and on from England to the Western Front. There are letters and cards, of course, but it's the parcels, wrapped in brown paper and knotted with twine, that fill the mailbags.

And all around those mailbags are people going home for Christmas. There are English soldiers and civil servants off back to their families.

Coming the other way, the boats are filled with people from every county in Ireland.

Some of them are prisoners, now released from jails where they have been interned, untried since the rebellion at Easter.

They are met on the quayside by exhilarated men and women who wave tricolours and shout: 'Up the Republic!'

Other travellers – also home for Christmas – have been working in England's farms and its factories. They are usually unmet, they just travel on by tram and train, home for a while before turning and going back.

The country they come home to is locked in a deep and brutal freeze – the 'worst in a generation, or maybe in two', say the newspapers.

Down in Midleton, the Christmas hunt has been cancelled.

Over in Co. Mayo, the proprietor of the Ballina Picture Palace has bought in the official film of the Battle of the Somme as the centrepiece of his Christmas programme. It is, he says, 'marvellous drama' which 'brings vividly before the mind all the terrible realities of war'.

But the snow and ice and repeated, bitter frosts make travel from country areas treacherous and the crowds are down.

The weather worsens again and, in the cities, there is chaos on the Saturday before Christmas. All of Dublin's public clocks have stopped.

The ground is frozen so solidly in Glasnevin Cemetery that only one burial is possible – and only when the gravediggers finally manage to split the soil with pickaxes. But other, peopled coffins are put in a vault and stored for a thaw.

Dublin's blacksmiths open early in the morning, every morning, but cannot cope with the demand to fix frost knives to the hooves of horses.

The unshod horses slip and slide and fall off roads and onto pathways. Hills are impossible to manage. Across the city, families are left without milk as daily deliveries are abandoned and fallen horses lie beside pools of milk.

Dublin Corporation is condemned for not sanding or salting as the traffic through the city dwindles and dies. Even the trams can only run patchily.

There is invention, however. Some women are spotted

edging along footpaths using long, iron-pointed poles to steady themselves. Some others walk to mass on Sunday morning with spare socks on the outside of their shoes.

But everywhere there are accidents – more than 300 people are brought to hospital in Dublin, having fallen on frozen streets. In country towns there are broken shoulders and concussed heads.

Some of those who are injured were out skating on the canals of the city. Indeed, all across the country people take to whatever river or canal or lake or pond they could half-trust and walk out onto them. People who had never had the chance before made impromptu skates and taught themselves the basics. Mostly, it ended well and people remembered for the rest of their lives the joy of skating.

But there is also tragedy. Out at Peamount Sanitorium, near Lucan to the west of Dublin, more than twenty patients skate on a frozen pond in a field adjoining Burns' Quarry. There is fun and laughter and childlike pleasure in the sharp air. Three of the skaters – John Flaherty, James Lynn and Michael Cannon – spin off across the ice. They race around and end in a happy embrace.

And then disaster: the skaters fall through the ice, into twelve feet of icy water. And disappear.

Five others rush to save them and they, too, end up in difficulty. Those five are saved only when the remaining patients make a rope of their coats and pull them to safety. Later that evening, the pond is dragged and the bodies of the three skaters are recovered. The watch in John Flaherty's pocket is stuck at 7pm – he was twenty-four, the eldest of the three who drowned.

The thaw comes. There's slush everywhere and broken pipes spewing water and the broken glass of milk bottles to be swept from the streets.

But it's Christmas week and the shops are open and people throng again into towns. Swantons in Nenagh have Christmas crackers and stockings to hang and all manner of 'fancy groceries' from plum puddings to wrapped-up chocolates.

The pantomimes are back rehearsing and the cinemas are filled. And the pubs are bursting with life – word is out that the price of a pint is to jump from four pence to five pence on 1 January and men are determined to fill the tank before then.

And more and more people are coming in off the boats. Some soldiers are home now from France and more rebels are home, too. They share the same boats as they pass in through Dublin Bay. The air is still cold, but the snow has passed and the gales have weakened.

Then, on Christmas morning, the last boat into Dublin carries men who have been in Reading Jail since July. These men have fought an empire – and will fight it again soon. There's Cathal O'Shannon and Terence MacSwiney, Seán T. O'Kelly and Ernest Blythe. They're laughing and singing, giddy with the idea of home – they were meant to be down in steerage, but have managed to push their way up into the first-class saloon. And there, now, in the middle of them is Tomás MacCurtain from Cork. He is playing the fiddle, as if his future and his freedom stretch endlessly in front of him. The sun is up when the men step off the boat and step into the city – into Christmas.

## Sunday, 21 January 1917

It's the morning of Sunday, 21 January 1917, the day of the war-delayed 1916 All-Ireland hurling final. The Tipperary hurlers are walking up O'Connell Street. All around them lies the wreckage of the Rising that had taken place the previous Easter. Whole stretches of buildings along Sackville Street – and along other streets leading off it – are now missing. The hurlers move down the street to the GPO. They gather silently in front of its ruins. And they recite a decade of the Rosary in honour of the rebels who had fought there.

They then head towards Croke Park where they are due to meet Kilkenny, the dominant power in hurling. This dominance was built between 1904 and 1913 when Kilkenny won seven All-Ireland championships. It was in these years that the famous black-and-amber jersey was adopted and photographs of those stripy men, sitting proudly on All-Ireland Sunday, hang on walls in family homes and public houses, in celebration of everyday heroes.

Kilkenny expects that today will bring another picture to be framed and nailed. The hurlers are predominantly from the Tullaroan club and they are led by the legendary Sim Walton. But the hurlers of Tipperary are also resolute in their confidence. They are almost all from the club of Boherlahan, a rural parish in south Tipperary, near Cashel. Men from that parish had won three All-Irelands in four years between 1896 and 1899, and such was their sense of themselves that they retired undefeated from competition after the 1898 All-Ireland final on the premise that, like Alexander the Great, they had no known worlds left to conquer.

The old blue and gold-banded jerseys that had been worn back in the 1890s have now been brought out again in 1917 for a new generation of hurlers.

These hurlers are led out onto the field of Croke Park by their captain, Johnny Leahy. Playing alongside him on the team is his brother Paddy.

Two of their brothers – Mick and Tommy – would later win All-Ireland medals. And a fifth brother – Jimmy – would be Officer Commanding of the 2nd Tipperary Brigade in the War of Independence.

The loss of the sight of one eye in an attack on Borrisoleigh Barracks during that war later restricted his hurling career but, in the time-honoured tradition of the lost brother always being the superior one, local observers would deem Jimmy to have been 'the handiest of them all'.

Now, though, as Johnny Leahy takes the field, it is a wet day and the ground is heavy.

The upshot is a merciless struggle, particularly in the early stages, with savage battles all across Croke Park. For sixteen minutes no score arrives. But then Tipperary score a goal and hats and caps are sent soaring skywards. The goal is enough to help them into a narrow half-time lead.

But, in the minutes after half-time, Kilkenny raise their game to a level which had already come to define them. They pummel Tipperary and the Tipp men seem to have no answer. The hurling, notes one journalist, is 'magnificent and thrilling in the extreme'.

Three goals flow in and Kilkenny now lead by five points with ten minutes to go.

A bookmaker working in the ground begins to shout

long odds against a Tipperary victory, but he will soon live to regret his rashness.

Led by Johnny Leahy, a Tipperary resurgence resting on relentless physical commitment turns the game on its head. Against scenes of unrestrained joy, they power through the Kilkenny defence and rattle in three goals of their own. It is enough to claim victory by 5–4 to 4–2.

A glorious feature of the game was the ferocity of the duel between the two captains. When the final whistle was blown the pair sought each other out and the verbal exchange became part of the lore of hurling finals.

'We were better hurlers than ye, Leahy,' said the Kilkenny captain, Sim Walton.

Johnny Leahy did not disagree but he was not without an answer. 'Yes,' he said, 'but we were the better men, Sim.'

The passage of time – and the momentous events of that decade – soon eased any strains that were generated on the field during that final.

Later, when Sim Walton wanted a safe house for Kilkenny Republicans on the run during the War of Independence, he brought them across the county boundary and into the home of his old adversary in Boherlahan, Johnny Leahy.

The two men sat around the kitchen table, and talked of hurling and farming and politics.

They stopped only when it was time for the cows to be milked and for Sim Walton to head back to Tullaroan.

They had hurled against each other in a time of war – but were bound together by the field that they had once shared and by their shared politics of revolution.

## Bloody Sunday, 1920

The real meaning of Bloody Sunday lies not in grand historical narratives but in the personal pain and the legacy of trauma of those who were bereaved.

How did Jerome O'Leary cope with the death of his young son, also called Jerome? He was just ten years of age and from 69 Blessington Street in Dublin. He was murdered as he sat on a wall behind the Canal End goal, watching the early stages of the match between the footballers of Dublin and Tipperary. His body was later identified at the Mater Hospital by his father who said simply: 'He was a schoolboy.'

How did Bridget Robinson cope with having to go on a Sunday evening from her house on Little Britain Street across to the old Drumcondra Hospital where her son William lay?

William had been sitting in a tree watching the match when a bullet ripped into his chest and out through his shoulder, throwing him to the ground. He fought to survive, but he could not be saved. Bridget Robinson, herself, was just twenty-nine and her dead son was eleven. How did she cope? And how did her husband Patrick cope with having been in that hospital as a surgeon fought to save the life of his son?

The events of Bloody Sunday in Croke Park quickly took on a national historical significance which eclipsed the suffering of the bereaved. This is what ordinarily happens in time of war: the rollcall of the dead is absorbed into the conflict.

Death becomes another thing to be fought over. Once that happens, reclaiming truth becomes almost impossible, and protecting the place of the people who lost their lives or who had their lives destroyed is undermined.

What happened in Croke Park on Bloody Sunday passed into the story of the Irish revolution. It became a key reference point, evidence of the brutality of the British regime, of callousness and cruelty, of disregard for the lives of the 'mere' Irish. It was the ultimate indictment of empire. And that the brutality of the murders in Croke Park was compounded by the crass denials and cover-ups that inevitably followed was further proof of what truly lay at the heart of British rule in Ireland.

Naturally, Bloody Sunday also became a touchstone in the history of the GAA. In independent Ireland, the legacy of Bloody Sunday included a real and genuine desire to remember those people who had been murdered at a Gaelic football match. The naming of the Hogan Stand – after Michael Hogan, the Tipperary player who died in a pool of blood on the field where he was supposed to be playing a game – and the subsequent unveiling of plaques were rooted in a sincere sense of loss.

But Bloody Sunday also got absorbed into the GAA's own history in a very particular way. It was pushed forward time and time again as compelling, incontrovertible evidence of the GAA's identification with the nationalist struggle which led to the establishment of the Irish Free State.

More than that, it also became something that could be thrown at the GAA's rivals. For example, down in Waterford in 1931 – in the midst of a dispute between the GAA and soccer – the chairman of the Waterford GAA county board, Willie Walsh, asked pointedly where the Rugby Union, the Soccer Association or the Hockey Association were on Bloody Sunday? He taunted that the Black and Tans had not gone to Dalymount Park or Lansdowne Road to look for rebels. Instead, it was at Croke Park that, he said, they 'performed deeds which shocked the civilised world. They knew friend from foe ...'

The backdrop to this insult was the enduring desire of the GAA to imagine that it was in the vanguard of the Irish revolution. The reality is much more complex – but the GAA constructed a history that sought to destroy that complexity. It ignored the fact that, after the 1916 Rising, its representatives had negotiated with the British commander in Ireland, General Sir John Maxwell, in an attempt to arrange for the provision of special trains to GAA matches. It sought also to disappear the fact that many GAA members had fought in the British army in the Great War.

All the while the lives of those who were bereaved were lived out as this new history was built around them. This was a cartoon history of goodies and baddies. And it was sanitised of the raw grief of bereavement.

But it is this grief that ties the day together. It unites Jerome O'Leary and Bridget Robinson with the family of Patrick MacCormack who had been shot dead by Irish Republicans in the Gresham Hotel on the morning of Bloody Sunday. He was an innocent horse dealer, shot in an apparent case of mistaken identity. In the rooms of the Gresham, it was said that the amount of blood was 'particularly shocking'; it soaked the carpet in deep crimson pools.

The blood of Bloody Sunday flowed freely through the day and its legacy left an appalling stain on the lives of too many people. It is in this remembrance, in the raw truth of grief and irrecoverable loss, that the true meaning of war can be found.

## The Nation

Nationalism allows people to wrap murder in a flag and present it as war in a just cause. It allows the ideologues of that cause to take history, scrub away the bits that do not fit the new fairytale, and write a version more fitted to their aims.

This is a thing we are well familiar with in Ireland – and yet, although we are good at pointing out the absurdities of those who do it in other lands, we do not want to recognise it in ourselves.

The context of all of this is the brutality of imperialism, the 'war capitalism' on which the empire was founded, the riches that flowed from its use of slavery, of expropriation of indigenous people and of the violence of its army. Irish nationalism must be considered within that frame of British imperialism.

Clearly, the manner in which sport was bound into empire inevitably coloured how it developed in Ireland.

In general, the influence of nationalism in sport is more benign than in politics, but it is real nonetheless. It is used by individuals and organisations to further their own success – whether measured in popularity or wealth – and in the process the past of a nation and its symbols are routinely subverted to this end.

You can see this in the manner in which Conor McGregor presents himself. From the flying of the tricolour to the singing of 'The Rocky Road', this is a man who rings the bells of his pay-per-view customers. You can see it, also, every time you walk into Croke Park and look over at Hill 16. No Irish sporting story better emphasises the manner in which history can be reconstructed to destroy truth.

The GAA had bought the old sportsground at Jones Road in 1913 and renovated large sections of it by 1915. Included in that renovation was the banking behind the Railway End goals. At precisely that moment the Royal Dublin Fusiliers were engaged in a ferocious battle at Gallipoli for possession of a hill between Suvla Bay and Anzac Cove during World War I; this hill was simply known as Hill 60. The fight for the hill lasted for an intense week in August 1915.

During that week and afterwards, Hill 60 was emblazoned in newspaper headlines and was documented in letters home from the front that were reprinted in the Dublin press. The redeveloped corner of Croke Park was considered to resemble the description of the embattled hill, and soon after, that part of the ground became known as Hill 60.

There was already precedence for this. Several English soccer grounds used the term Spion Kop (or Kop for short) to describe their terraces; the logic was that their steep nature was evocative of a hill near Ladysmith, South Africa, where the Battle of Spion Kop was fought in January 1900 during the Second Boer War. This happened at soccer grounds such as Anfield and Hillsborough. Back in Dublin, newspaper reportage on GAA matches through the 1920s regularly noted the great crowds which congregated on Hill 60, with the *Irish Independent* noting in September 1925 that it was 'a living mountain of human faces'. It is not just the Dublin papers that referred to it as Hill 60; the same was the case for local papers such as the *Munster Express* and the *Connacht Tribune*.

The use of the name Hill 60 was a matter of disquiet to some members of the GAA and surfaced publicly for the first time at a meeting of the Central Council of the association in September 1931. Dan McCarthy, a veteran of the 1916 Rising and former president of the GAA, said that he took exception to the use of the name Hill 60. He said that Croke Park was 'sacred ground ... sanctified by the blood of martyrs.' In this, of course, McCarthy was referring to the events of Bloody Sunday. The fight for Irish freedom should be commemorated, McCarthy argued, rather than one that 'took place in a foreign country', fought by a foreign army. In response to McCarthy's words, the secretary of the GAA told the meeting that he had already drawn the attention of newspapers to the matter. The meeting agreed that whenever the name Hill 60 was used in the press, the GAA would make plain to editors the association's disapproval. Finally, McCarthy said that they should call it Hill 16, in obvious homage to the revolution, but that if they couldn't do that they should find some other appropriate title.

They called it Hill 16.

Advertisements around matches now set out the charges for spectators entering Hill 16. The pressure on the newspapers to change the name was also successful. In September 1931, the same month of the GAA meeting where McCarthy had raised his objections to the Hill 60 name, *The Irish Press* newspaper was published for the first time. It always referred to Hill 16; only once did it mistakenly use the term Hill 60 in connection with Croke Park, and even then the paper apologised the following day.

The mood of the times was clear and was underlined when the Cusack Stand was opened in August 1938, named in honour of the founder of the GAA, Michael Cusack. Speaking at the official opening, the then-president of the GAA, Pádraig MacNamee said in a speech that Hill 16 was 'an ever constant reminder of the gallant band who made the supreme sacrifice that this land of theirs might be Gaelic and free'.

That more GAA men had fought for the British army during the Great War – including at Gallipoli – than had been in the GPO during the 1916 Rising was simply written out of history, an inconvenient fact that needed now to be ignored.

Along with a new name came a myth to go with it: Hill 16 was claimed to have been built from the rubble of the 1916 Rising. It appears that this myth was first aired in the 1930s; it was certainly mentioned in a letter from 'Two Gaels' to the editor of the *Meath Chronicle*. These men, in urging Meath to victory in an All-Ireland final in 1939, noted that the team would be facing the tricolour that would fly above Hill 16 during the playing of the national anthem 'in respect to Ireland's fallen heroes, whose blood stain the debris in that immortal hill'.

This invention eventually hardened into fact: Hill 16 had been built from the rubble of the 1916 Rising. Best of all, a living witness to it all emerged through the thick smoke of a Dublin pub: a man who not only knew for a fact it had happened, but had actually helped make it happen. In the

*Sunday Independent,* journalist Raymond Smith wrote in his weekly column in January 1966 that he had met an old Dubliner in a pub on Middle Abbey Street. As he drank his pint, the man told Smith that he had been paid 6d a load for transporting the rubble up from O'Connell Street to Croke Park.

History was overwhelmed by the power of men in pubs telling stories. We could all now pretend that Hill 16 had only ever been Hill 16, and that no GAA man had ever served in the British army or in the RIC. Because, of course, the cause demands that all that is inconvenient must be wished away and a new truth constructed.

# 8 PLACE

In September 1957, Vincent Kehoe left New York for Spain to make a film about bullfighting, and to simultaneously write a book. He travelled across the country, shooting 12,000 feet of film and taking over 5,000 photographs. What emerged was a deeply respectful, even awestruck account of what he described as 'an art form of the highest order'. What happened in a bullring, he wrote, was 'more than just a fight', rather a higher art where 'a man faces death by daring an animal bred specifically to attack anything that moves. Only by his skill and a cloth cape does the man manage to deflect the animal's attention from himself.' Properly understood, it is 'not a contest of equally balanced elements but of entirely different ones. It is not a game or sport with sides and scoring, but a display of unreasoning brute force and untamed fury pitted against the seemingly feeble, but generally successful, thinking action of a man.'

Rather than being about bullfighting, however, Kehoe's book is more than anything a study of place. He uses bullfighting to explore the small towns of southern Spain, places where the arena of the fight was the town itself.

Kehoe recorded how bullfights were held for local fiestas when there was a Holy Day or an annual *feria* (fair); local youths performed with younger animals in portable arenas or barricaded town squares. In 1958, while Kehoe worked his way across Spain, three men lost their lives in accidents connected with bullfighting – one in the ring itself, the others in ancillary events. Kehoe saw in this loss evidence of a deep connection between play and the people of a place: 'This is the theatre of life and death. It is drama in its highest form – classic tragedy.' The pressure to perform was immense. In one of the bullfights of 1958, a new bullfighter panicked and refused to fight: he was arrested for cowardice and fined 1,000 pesetas, a significant sum of money at that time.

Such extremes of emotion as are revealed in the work of Vincent Kehoe do not need to be manifest for us to understand the quotidian relationship between sport and place. This relationship works in many different ways, each unique unto its own geography. It is a simple truth that every sport needs a place and time. When that place becomes a venue for sport, it invariably creates a lore. This is a lore which is added to layer by layer, generation by generation. But it can also be a lore that is made new or renewed, something that can grow immediately and powerfully. Even if a place disappears as somewhere to play, the memories live on. As Seamus Heaney wrote in 'The Strand':

> The dotted line my father's ashplant made
> On Sandymount Strand
> Is something else the tide won't wash away.

## Dollymount Strand

When you turn right off the Howth Road, coming out from Dublin city, and cross the wooden bridge onto the North Bull Wall, the sheer diversity of the world of sport announces itself.

That the North Bull Wall should exist at all is, in itself, a tale which edges towards the incredible. It seems to be the case that the idea for building the Bull Wall came from William Bligh, the famous captain of the HMS Bounty. The plan was to do something to deepen the shallow water of the bay and to deal with the sandbacks that were so hazardous to the expanding trade that was coming into Dublin Port in the eighteenth century.

The wall was duly completed using granite and limestone, and was ready by 1824. It improved the port – and has improved the lives of generations of Dubliners since then.

Now, as you pass down the Bull Wall promenade, you come to two modernist concrete bathing shelters, built in the 1930s. They are a legacy of the commitment that Dublin Corporation had to providing simple public amenities.

There is no doubt that the capacity of the corporation was limited by the resources at its disposal, and by the prioritisation of other needs, but there is something wonderful about the bathing shelters.

Apart from anything else, they stand as monuments to hope – the hope that a scorching summer would see them teem with people escaping into the water and enjoying the pleasure of a swim.

But even now, with autumn turning to winter, there are people in the sea. They have stripped to their swimming togs

– no sign of a wetsuit – and walked down the stone steps into the icy sea and are now drifting around in the water.

The wind has whipped up and the sea is choppy behind them as it stretches back across the bay towards the Great South Wall, Ringsend and the prosperous coastal suburbs of Blackrock and Dun Laoghaire.

People have swum in this sea for as long as people have lived on the island, but when you pass further along the promenade and slip across onto Dollymount Strand, a much more modern sport is on view.

More than two dozen kitesurfers are making use of the strengthening wind to shoot up and down the shallow water at speeds touching 60kmph.

Kite surfing has become one of the fastest growing water sports in Ireland. The season runs March to November, but these are nominal limits. If the weather is in any way suitable, kitesurfers take their kits and their boards to the beach.

On Dollymount Strand it is an extraordinary sight.

The wind pulls the surfers faster and faster and they shoot into the air off waves, twisting and turning, before making water again.

In some respects, this is a rejection of the formal world of sport. It is a sport whose participants organise themselves as a community rather than a club. It is not competitive in the sense of people competing against each other (except for the very exceptional few who are international adventure sports stars).

The sport grew out of surfing, windsurfing and other adventure sports in the last decades of the twentieth century.

The arrival of major windsurfing manufacturers into the sport around the turn of the millennium saw it move towards the mainstream and within a decade the sport had spread to coastal areas around the world.

Here on Dollymount there are Irish men and women who have taken up the sport in recent years. And all around them are Poles and Lithuanians, a German and a woman from South America.

The idea that kitesurfing will become a medalling sport in the Olympics feels entirely at odds with what is on view on Dollymount Strand. The lure of money is massive, of course, but it would be a shame if something as joyous as kitesurfing could end up grist to the mill of the International Olympic Committee.

The thing about Dollymount, of course, is that its great expanse allows for recreation of many types. There are people walking their dogs – or just walking themselves – up and down the strand.

There are two toddlers throwing sand at each other and roaring laughter. A father and son are kicking a ball to each other and at four different places, there's a sliotar being pucked over and across.

Right in the middle of the beach, a young girl – not yet a teenager – is bouncing a ball on her hurley and striking it in the air. It's rhythmic and her timing is perfect, as she counts away in Polish: 'Jeden ... dwa ... trzy ... cztery ... pięć ...'

The way she plays and the way the whole strand is a free site for people to enjoy whatever form of recreation they prefer is a reminder that sport is much more than the formal structures of clubs and their codified games.

Yet clubs and associations are a fundamental part of the story of the North Bull.

Walking back out along the promenade, down to the right – with Howth Head standing majestic in the background – sits the Royal Dublin Golf Club. The links were designed by H.S. Colt, a world-famous golf architect, back in the 1920s. It is celebrated as one of the great links courses in the world and when it hosted the Irish Open between 1983 and 1985, the competition was won once by Bernhard Langer and twice by Seve Ballesteros.

The Royal Dublin Club, itself, however, is older than its links. It was actually founded at rooms at 19 Grafton Street in 1885 by John Lumsden, the manager of the College Street branch of the Provincial Bank.

Lumsden, along with two of his sons, laid down a golf course at the Phoenix Park, near the Viceregal Lodge (now Áras an Uachtaráin) and played away there before, ultimately, the move out to its current home.

Now, the Royal Dublin Golf Club has a barrier across the entrance to its carpark and a large sign instructing all that it is 'Private Property'. You need serious disposable income to be able to afford its membership – it has a formal structure in the way that kitesurfing does not.

This is not to set one off against the other, as some sort of binary opposition. The great thing about sport and recreation is that there is something for just about everyone.

For those who wish to follow the inherited traditions of modern sport, there is a clear way of doing so. For those who escape from the mainstream, there are everchanging options of finding fun in play.

## Phibsboro

'Come on to fuck Rovers!' came the roar fifteen minutes after half-time from a man buried somewhere in the middle of the Sligo fans.

It was easy to see what inspired that roar.

Sligo Rovers were in Dalymount Park to play Bohemians in the Airtricity League and they started both halves as comfortably the better team.

But – in the second half as in the first – they just faded away; it was as if the early superiority was something that they didn't really believe in.

The Sligo fan could sense the game slipping away through the lack of a cutting-edge and he was right: his team lost – and they deserved to lose. Kurtis Byrne drove a magnificent shot to the roof of the Sligo net and the *Great Book of Sporting Clichés* demands that it be described as a moment worthy of winning any match.

After the game, as both sets of supporters applauded their teams from the field, there was no rancour in defeat, no raucousness in victory. The honesty of effort from the players was appreciated by all.

The thing is, of course, that it was not just the match that brought people to Dalymount Park.

This was also about tradition and loyalty and belonging and community.

It was about the thrill of promise.

That is the undying thrill that comes from walking to a football ground as the night closes in and there's a little sharpness in the air. From far away, you could see the glow of the floodlights and hear the hum of noise that flows from gathering crowds and ageing tannoy systems.

The walk into Dalymount Park was like something from a comic book of Victorian England: a narrow lane ran between rows of red-brick houses and even a smallish crowd felt like a big one under the darkness at the rear of the main stand.

All around were relics of the past. The old turnstiles were made in Manchester, at a time when the north of England was the workshop of the world. It was easy to imagine that these turnstiles clicked away on Saturday afternoons as thousands of flat-capped men pushed through to see Oldham or Bolton play.

In the tunnels under the main stand, the pictures of former greats hung proudly and the bars at either end were full – and full of fun.

This was Bohemians' first home match of the season and the atmosphere was a warm one. All around the main stand people were greeting each other and catching up after the close-season.

That stand underlined the extent to which Dalymount Park was filled with people who love their club and are proud of it and of its place in the life of north inner-city Dublin.

But Dalymount is, of course, much more than that: it was – for more than half a century – the place where Ireland played its home international soccer matches.

Nostalgia for that era drips off Colin White's fine book *Dalymount Park: The Home of Irish Football.*

When you look at the photographs of twelve decades of soccer played on that field, wedged between Phibsboro and Cabra, it is easy to understand how it became the epicentre of the lives of intertwining generations.

The presence of Pelé and Bobby Moore and John Giles and a whole host of local League of Ireland stars obviously offered an attraction that re-invented itself year after year as new heroes were made.

But the backdrop to almost every black-and-white photograph in the book is a crowd of a scale that can only be dreamed of today. Those rows and rows of spectators must have been an attraction in themselves – there is no way that people stood there just to watch the play; the magic of crowds is potent and magnetic.

The surge and sway of a terrace as the net ripples is one of the unique sights of sport that is no longer seen in soccer on these islands.

The remnants of that era are all too apparent today. The crumbling terrace behind the goal to the right of the main stand was empty – apart from one ball-boy who pushed over the weeds to retrieve the wildest shots.

The opposite side of the ground was also empty – apart from the cars that sat where people once stood.

Down to the left, the old Shed leaned over newish seating (also empty) as if to cast a shadow on the present, a reminder of the way things once were.

It is easy to come to Dalymount Park and be swallowed up by its history, by the faded grandeur of its glory days. It is also easy to lament the enduring failures of the soccer authorities in Ireland to invest in its facilities, and to create and sustain a league that matches the passion of its people. It is easy, most of all, to dismiss the prospect of this ever really changing for the better.

But there is enough in Dalymount Park on a Friday

night – and enough in soccer clubs all around Ireland – to fashion a future. It will not be easy, but it comes down to organisation and sustainable development. The follies of the past – ridiculous wages, madcap speculation and the capacity to blame everyone else for Irish soccer's woes – have no place in such a future.

The plans for the future development of Dalymount Park are serious and their realisation is relatively imminent. The fact that the state and Dublin City Council are involved offers a ballast without which the proposed stadium would most likely remain a fiction.

The development of this stadium also creates a challenge for Bohemians. For all that Dalymount Park has grievously decayed, it retains a genuine charm as a sort of glorious wreck. Alongside this charm is a homeliness that is fundamental and compelling. Too many modern stadiums are off-the-shelf, synthetic and soulless – Bohemians can't allow that to happen to their home.

# 9 SCHOOL

If it is accepted that the child is the father of the man, then it is also the case that the classroom is central to that fathering. There is a groove that runs from a classroom in Tullamore CBS in September 1982 through to the present. The memories of my schooldays in the 1980s and the friendships that have endured across the decades run along that groove. This is not a matter of nostalgia – or, at least, it's not just a matter of nostalgia. It was not a school that was overburdened with resources: there was no gym, no changing rooms for the fields, no educational facilities beyond the very basic. But there were brilliant teachers and I had the good fortune to land in a class that suited me. Some of those teachers who taught me are still working in the school. It is a pleasure to go back there to teach a class. It is now a modern, vibrant school with great facilities and a new generation of teachers. The atmosphere is good – you can always tell a school by the atmosphere that hangs in the air. It's hard to define exactly what it is, except to say that you recognise it best when it is missing.

And the boys in that school now? They are much the same as we were. There is a lot of talk about how different children are now from even ten or twenty years ago. This is mostly due to the fact that they are a generation who have never known life without a computer or the internet. They live in a digital globalised world and they live in that world through the filter of computing devices. But to define the boys just by the context of their lives is wrong; just as it would be wrong to define my generation by the context of growing up in a brutal recession where emigration seemed inevitable. It matters, but it is not everything. Standing now in the classrooms in that school, it is a joy to be slagged by the students, to get the look that says *What would you know, old man?*

And yet, they wear the same colour jerseys and play on the same pitches we did.

## Fifth Year Boys

It's July 1985. Three women are walking past a grotto in the small West Cork village of Ballinspittle. The grotto is a beautiful one, set back into the hillside and surrounded by bushes. The women stop to pray and as they pray they see the statue of the Virgin Mary come alive. Later that evening, a dozen more people say that they, also, have seen the statue of the Virgin Mary in Ballinspittle move.

News of this moving statue is reported first by the local press, and then the national and international press.

Thousands of people begin congregating every evening. Hymns are sung and prayers recited; many claim to see the statue move. Minor miracles are reported: a woman cured of deafness; a stroke victim cured of paralysis.

Within weeks, one-quarter of a million people are reported to have made their way to Ballinspittle, Co. Cork to see its moving statue and to pray.

Then, as summer turns to autumn, other statues in other parishes begin to move as crowds congregate at Marian shrines all across Ireland.

Down in Offaly, the classroom of 5A in Tullamore CBS is full of boys waiting for anything to happen.

There's a geography class being taught by Seamus O'Dea, the school vice-principal.

Behind him is a blackboard and above the blackboard is a two-foot high statue of the Virgin Mary, in flowing blue-and-white robes and a strange red-lipped smile.

'She's moving, sir. She definitely moved.'

'Sit down Cooney – it's not feeding time yet,' says Mr O'Dea.

'But, sir, I saw it too. She's swaying.'

'Should you ring RTÉ, sir?'

All down the rows of the classroom boys are staring up at the statue, trying to look angelic and awestruck, overacting in magnificent piety, their desks remade as altars.

Seamus O'Dea is doing his best not to laugh. He knows he can't turn around to look up at the statue – that would be to hand a victory to a room he must not lose to.

But, anyway, he likes our class and he knows we like him and we're no real trouble so he won't go hard on us.

He also knows that this, too, will pass. Although, in the way of these things, we will not let it pass until it has been well and happily milked.

'She just waved at me, sir.'

'Sir, she's breakdancing now.'

On it goes like that for class after class, trying to get a rise out of the teachers, trying to get the day just to move along so that we can escape into the air.

Someone makes a homemade 'Out of Order' sign and hangs it around Mary's shoulders. It disappears when we go home for the evening.

The next day, a new sign is made. It reads: 'Insert coin'. That, too, disappears into the empty evening.

Then the miracle happens.

The Virgin Mary has been very carefully pushed – by a boy or boys – to the edge of the shelf above the blackboard. It will surely fall the first time any teacher takes a duster to the board.

Fall it does – a sort of premonition of Morrissey singing 'alabaster crashes down'. The statue hits the floor with a huge thump. It must shatter.

But it doesn't – the Virgin Mary stays in one piece, apparently unharmed.

'A miracle, sir. A miracle!'

'She jumped, sir. With no parachute!'

Back down in Ballinspittle, a Garda sergeant has seen the statue move. He later recounts: 'I saw the concrete statue of Our Lady floating in mid-air. Not rocking to and fro but floating. Rosaries were being said, hymns were being sung. Suddenly, without warning, it was as if the statue simply took off and became airborne.'

There can be no denying the sincerity of his words – or of the genuine belief in a church whose privileged place was now being increasingly undermined by the way the world was changing and undermined by itself.

But faith in a moving statue is also a reminder that if you look at something long enough, you can end up seeing whatever it is you wish to see.

Looking back into the 1980s, looking through the schoolgates, past the wedgie tree and the smoking shed and lads playing handball in the morning and basketball after school, I see a room full of boys. There are big white boot runners and mullets and flecky trousers and a wall full of green parkas. There's learning and laughter and messing and gear bags with dirty football boots. Nobody has a clue what's happening. All the days have been squeezed into one endless class lost in the fog of adolescence.

The Virgin Mary is standing on top of the blackboard.

And we are all waiting.

## Too Many Mondays

Being a schoolboy in a classroom full of Liverpool fans during the 1980s was a painful experience. It's the kind of pain that causes scarring that never clears.

They were everywhere, sitting at every desk, sneering, superior, endlessly smug. And that is just to mention the nicer ones.

All the Mondays of that tortuous decade merge into one long and brutal recounting of another Saturday's play where Liverpool had casually rolled over whichever pretenders stood in their way.

Dalglish. Rush. Whelan. Hansen. Lawrenson. All sickeningly brilliant. All so relentlessly successful that you could imagine them out playing pitch-and-toss with their medals against the back wall of the Kop.

Liverpool dominated the league, of course; seemed to be champions in perpetuity, and then went around Europe beating everyone while barely breaking sweat, as if on a glorious, leisurely bus tour of the continent.

Each of these successes brought the carving of freshly triumphant slogans into the soft wood of the school desks. But, of course, desks alone could never have been enough of a canvas for the lads in our class. They wrote also on the copy books and rulers and pencil cases and everything else they could find belonging to the few Manchester United supporters in the room. I had 'LFC' tippexed onto my schoolbag and jacket in huge letters by one particularly devout specimen. The fine job he works in now cannot disguise the monster that lurks within.

All the while, naturally, United flattered to deceive year after year, before always, always losing just when it mattered most.

A new United team would start a season well, backboned by some seriously good players – and then the couple of new players who had been introduced to turn challengers into champions would be revealed to be not nearly good enough. Or just flakey. Or both.

Off it would start again.

The worst was the 1985/6 season when United won the first ten games in a row and seemed set fair to canter to league glory. By the end of September they were nine points clear of Liverpool – at a time when a win was worth just two points.

There was solid evidence that there was no need to spare the return gloating. Indeed, it was in no way spared – rather it was mixed freely with taunts, gibes, liberal insults and a general obnoxiousness that seemed at the time to be only fair and proper.

At the beginning of October, United drew against Luton Town on their plastic pitch. They were still top at Christmas but the gap had shrunk to just two points and the inevitability of United's doom was apparent everywhere.

In the end, Liverpool won a league and cup double. United's star striker Mark Hughes signed for Barcelona. The Liverpool supporters in our class were truly appalling. Their taunting was relentless – there was no escape.

It wasn't just the winning that was the problem. In an interesting book he has written on the meaning of soccer, the philosopher Simon Critchley – himself a diehard Liverpool fan, although now based in New York – wrote: 'All my family came from Liverpool, and although there was an Evertonian wing in my mother's family, LFC always predominated. I was raised with a fanatical devotion to LFC and a belief that my team was not just very good, but that its fans were special and its culture unique.

'I know how irritating this can be to fans of other teams, because LFC supporters always seem so self-righteous and to think that what happened to them happened first/better/more intensely/more profoundly than elsewhere.'

That's exactly the way they were. And still are.

In fairness to Critchley, he did agree immediately that such sentiments are 'obviously completely delusional and empirically wrong'.

Why did English soccer matter so much to us in the 1980s?

After all, Offaly were winning All-Irelands in football and hurling, and Tullamore CBS was a school given mostly to Gaelic football. It was played all the time and the school had good teams.

There was hurling, also, but it was dwarfed by Gaelic football.

There was also basketball and table tennis and handball, all played in a recreational way, with flexible rules (all of which included permission to hit a fella a slap, at random, the only logic seemingly needed was that the opportunity presented itself).

There was no rugby played in the school and very little talked about – except, maybe, during the Five Nations. Even then, it didn't really matter a whole pile.

On the other hand, soccer mattered a lot. Very few actually played the game in organised teams, instead just kicking around in the schoolyard or at home in pick-up games.

But what happened on the soccer grounds of England shaped every week of the school year – and to be a Liverpool fan in those years was to live a gilded life.

The triumph of Manchester United in the Premier League era came too late. It needed to happen a decade earlier for it to have been a true gift.

By then, I had made the journey from supporter to mere sympathiser; without the context of the school classroom it just didn't matter enough. The meaning of English soccer was to be found in the slagging.

Against that there was the pure joy of watching Liverpool become what United had once been.

They were now the team who bought the wrong players, looking always for the alchemy that would restore former glories.

They also did things that were ridiculous. The best was the wearing of the white suits to the 1996 FA Cup Final. What must it have been like to put back on that suit after losing 1–0 to an Eric Cantona volley after being bullied around the pitch by Roy Keane?

That was a grand day – but it was spoiled by not being able to go into a classroom on the Monday morning and rub it in to those who had inflicted so many years of suffering.

# 10 FAMILY

I met Cormac McAnallen outside the toilet between two of the carriages on the train from Westport to Dublin. We both had got on at Tullamore station and were now sitting on our gearbags. It was not glamorous. He had just played for Tyrone against Offaly in O'Connor Park in front of 10,000 people, and I'd played a club match for Tullamore across the road in O'Brien Park in front of about 9,950 fewer. We ended up chatting for the hour and a half it took to get to Dublin. He was a really interesting man, intelligent and decent and unafraid of saying what he thought. Mostly, what was striking was how fair he was. There had been a few controversial incidents in the match between Tyrone and Offaly. An Offaly player had got the line. Cormac explained why he thought it was unfair. Although he did point also out that he had been in no great rush to point it out to the referee. Later, I got to know his brother Dónal and would like to consider him a friend. Dónal is a man who is brave, intellectual, kind and honourable. The way the two lads were as brothers was not much different to the way my brothers and I were with each other growing up. The connection was blood and place and play.

This bind of family changes when it crosses generations. What binds parent to child and child to parent is of course different to what binds siblings together. Explaining precisely this difference is not easy, and of course it shifts across families. But sport allows for family relationships. It is memories of going to matches together, playing games, practicing together, hitting a ball or kicking it, hours spent together. This is basically shared sporting experiences as part of the real-time experiment of living under the same roof.

## The McAnallen Brothers

There are things that a book can do for you that defy adequate explanation. It is a something deeply personal, a connection made with the words that lingers long after the book is closed and laid down. Such books are rare and when they are found they deserve to be cherished.

In the millions of words that have been written about the GAA and its players, there are surprisingly few outstanding books. How is it that a passion which is so central to the lives of so many has brought such a limited literature? And that in a country in which writing and writers are so celebrated.

Most of the books written around the GAA and its players are devoid of serious ambition. They are autobiographical works essentially driven by commerce and branding.

The very best of such books can be entertaining and informative, it is true. Usually, they open a crack and give a glimpse behind a dressing-room door and into the thinking of a particular player or manager. Usually, too, they tease rather than reveal, offering the illusion of insight; the author is always too loyal or too cute to really take a chisel to any doors. Theirs is a world where anecdote trumps revelation at almost every turn.

This is entirely understandable – who wants anyone else to know everything about them?

Very occasionally a book steps beyond these constraints. Two such GAA books are Breandán Ó hEithir's 1984 book, *Over the Bar: A Personal Relationship with the GAA* and Patrick Deeley's *The Hurley Maker's Son* (2016).

The success of both of those books lies in the way in which they transcend the individual. Instead, of being spancelled to the rehearsal of great games or particular controversies, they locate a personal story within a much broader frame of reference. Basically, they tell you as much about the world as they do about the individual.

Dónal McAnallen's beautiful *Pursuit of Perfection: The Life, Death and Legacy of Cormac McAnallen* must now be set alongside that shortlist of exceptional books. It is unique and compelling, raw and moving.

\* \* \*

Cormac McAnallen was born in February 1980. He lived in a house three miles from the village of Eglish in rural south-east Co. Tyrone, with his parents Brendan and Bridget, and his two brothers: Dónal who was eighteen months older and Fergus who was eighteen months younger.

The story of his early life is one familiar to boys all across Ireland – and, indeed, across much of the western world. He loved sport and comics and television programmes such as *Knight Rider*. He played marbles and climbed trees and got mucky. He went to school and worked hard there and had the sort of curious mind that reveled in the pursuit of knowledge.

But there was another aspect to this childhood that was absolutely unique to the locality: four people were killed in the Troubles in the week that he was born. The wider context here was 'partition, Stormont misrule and neglect'.

Cormac's Uncle Dan had been killed in 1973 while taking part in an attack on Pomeroy police station. Dan had been a football fanatic and had led an apolitical life before being radicalised by the civil rights movement and by the violent reaction of the government of Northern Ireland.

In the McAnallen household, Dan was not forgotten, but nor was his death allowed to define those who remained. Brendan and Bridget McAnallen made a conscious decision to steer their boys in a different direction: 'Martyrs have begotten martyrs in Irish history and they did not want to mourn another one. Immersion in local historical, cultural and sporting affairs would surely keep us safe. We should live for Ireland, not die for her.'

\*\*\*

The backdrop of repeated car searches and the passage of soldiers along country lanes and through their fields could never be normalised, but against this backdrop a passion for football was flowering.

Using posts cut from nearby trees, they made a pitch out of a back lawn. Sometimes Fergus (who had other interests than his two brothers) or their father or a cousin would kick with them, but usually it was Cormac and Dónal. Rugby during the Five Nations, tennis during Wimbledon, bits of hurling, but Gaelic football all year round.

In general, the portrait that is drawn of the childhood that ensued on that lawn and in the house and in forays beyond the gates (France and America, as well as across the border to Dublin and Donegal) is vivid and real. Layers of detail are placed one on top of the next. Usually, such layers are the product of memories or half-memories, old family tales and stories that have been burnished over time to fit a certain narrative.

Not in this book. The depth of its telling is made possible by the type of household Cormac McAnallen was reared in. It is true that sport was vital. The boys played football, of course, but also played other games ranging from cards and chess to snooker, table tennis and basketball. They raced around fields and undertook assault courses. They were restless and full of energy and the sort of vigour that makes a house bounce.

But alongside sport, this was a house where books and reading were essential. Inspired by their mother, the boys read everything from serious books borrowed from the library to comics such as *The Beano, Roy of the Rovers* and *Shoot!* The range of reading material serves as a reminder that it is not so much important what a child reads, rather that the child reads at all. There is something very lovely about the fact that the zenith of this comic-reading saw some fourteen comics coming into the house in any given week.

Partly from all of this reading grew a meticulous approach to documenting what was happening in the world around them and to record-keeping. For his part, Dónal ultimately became a pioneering historian whose work on the GAA, broadly, and on Ulster, in particular, is of the highest quality and underpinned by meticulous research.

But Cormac, too, wrote page after page through his formative years. His diaries form the bedrock of this book. To read these diary entries is to gain a special insight of how the boy grew into the man.

Sometimes the entries are funny, especially the boyish ones. In February 1987, for example, he noted that his father passed thirty-one cars heading into Omagh for a league match between Derry and Tyrone, while being passed themselves by just two!

At that same match, the name Cormac McAnallen was read out over the tannoy system for the first time ever: he had got lost when he wandered away to buy himself a packet of crisps.

All told, the entries record school and sport and family living and the everyday things that shape a life. They reveal the personality that was being forged and the impulses that drove him onwards. And they offer an extraordinary insight into the way he prepared for matches, how he thought about those matches, how he conquered himself and sought to win.

Without these diaries, this book could not work in the way that it does.

\* \* \*

Cormac's progress through the various levels of GAA competitions was relentless. For club and school and then for county and college, he emerged as a player who was fearless, skilful and utterly determined.

What stands out most of all is his love of play. It is this love that, more than anything, explains the dedication he brought to his craft. It explains, also, how he moved from being not just the outstanding player in his own age group, but also in the age group above his own.

He benefitted from the timing of his arrival. His boyhood progress was facilitated by the impetus given to Gaelic football in Tyrone in the wake of reaching the All-Ireland final of 1986. The improved structures that were built in the county produced a team good enough to reach another final in 1995.

The pain of that defeat, in turn, drove the making of a new team, one that would build on the achievements of the past, but one which would also learn from its failures.

There were many disappointments, setbacks and difficult days. But Tyrone were climbing up the mountain when Cormac arrived and his arrival, in itself, helped make that climb possible.

That Cormac McAnallen won Young Footballer of the Year, won an All-Star and was a key player as Tyrone won its first ever All-Ireland senior football championship underlines just how good he was.

But, while the story of the making of a brilliant footballer is obviously important to this book, it does not dominate unduly. There was too much else to his life to allow for that to be the case. Moving away to university, falling in love, training to be a teacher, working as a teacher – basically, doing the things that so many people do. All the while playing football, making himself better, striving for perfection.

\*\*\*

Running through this book is the deep love of one brother for another. This is a love that is portrayed on page after page. Sometimes it is apparent through apparently mundane details, the stuff of every family in which siblings like each other. In other times, it is made clear through manifestations of friendship and kinship and the sheer pleasure of spending time together.

Perhaps the most brilliant sentence in the book – and one that in its simplicity reveals so much about the lives of brothers who share passions – is the very first one: 'Cormac was always there.'

That's it, when it comes down to it. For Dónal McAnallen, his brother Cormac was in his world from his very first memory, breathing the same air, competing with him, sharing with him, helping him.

They shaped each other in so many ways and yet one of the most commendable aspects of the book is the determination of the author to make it understood that his brother was no plaster saint.

When as nice and successful a man as Cormac McAnallen dies at so young an age and in such circumstances, the temptation to present his life as a sort of perfection would be understandable. It is to the credit of Dónal McAnallen that he does not make that mistake. He shared too much with his brother for too long not to know that the perfect state of grace that no human being can achieve was also denied to his brother.

So it is that, for example, he describes Cormac as a 'dirty fib-dog' for writing as a young boy that the family had been to see *101 Dalmatians* in the cinema. No such trip was made and Dónal gently pointed out the invention.

Cormac fought, too: a scrap in the schoolyard saw him have his hair pulled while he tore the other boy's jumper. The result was six slaps from the master: corporal punishment was about to be consigned to history but in the 1980s it still reigned supreme in Irish schools.

Of course, there are the inevitable feelings that are provoked when the lives of brothers are pulled a little apart from each other when they grow out of their childhood. It is a tribute to the candour and courage of this book that this is met head on. It is not easy to be the brother of a county player who is not just a star in his own county but increasingly a 'media darling'. In short, Dónal became 'Cormac's brother'.

But Dónal, too, would have loved to have been a county footballer and doesn't shirk from saying that the loss of this dream was hard to take. He didn't begrudge Cormac a thing (the complete opposite, in fact), but the very fact of taking a different path brought a little distance.

Dónal was a little more bookish and had chosen never to drink. Cormac enjoyed a few drinks – and missing weekends – as he celebrated county success as an All-Ireland winning minor.

But this adjustment to growing up and growing a little apart does not take from the love that was shared between two boys whose lives were intertwined by being so alike, so close in age, growing up in a house where their parents did so much for them.

Underpinning everything was an unspoken bond, revealed most dramatically in two meetings (neither of which would be possible in the new age of elite posturing in Croke Park) in the minutes after Tyrone won the 2003 All-Ireland football final. Dónal led the charge onto the field after Tyrone had won and ran straight into Cormac; later, he managed to make his way into the Tyrone dressing-room. There were 'embraces, emotions and effusions'. Of these two encounters, Dónal writes: 'Cormac probably sensed in those two encounters, more than any words I'd ever say, how proud he made me.'

\*\*\*

Of course, with such depth of love comes a pain that is almost unbearable.

That pain, an unspeakable grief, visited the McAnallen house in March 2004 when Cormac died in his bed in the middle of the night.

Dónal heard the death-rattle and rushed to Cormac's room. The house woke and worked frantically to revive him. An ambulance and a retired local doctor was summoned. It was to no avail. The words of their father set out the grim brutality of it all: 'I think the poor child's dead.'

The days, the weeks, the years after the death are handled in the book with great care. The new reality in all its appalling detail had to be dealt with in the public eye.

For Cormac's new fiancée Ashlene, for his parents, for his brothers, for the wider family, the flood of grief, the incomprehension, the raw crushing agony was endured in the open as well as in private.

The funeral was a 'maelstrom'. The immediate aftermath saw the BBC air a tribute documentary. Asked by interviewer Jerome Quinn what he would say to Cormac if he had a chance, Dónal said with overwhelming poignancy: 'Tar ar ais' ('Come back').

\* \* \*

Cormac McAnallen is now dead for almost as long a time as he lived. The memory of his deeds is a vivid one. The impact on the life of a loving family is still apparent. As Dónal writes: 'What hits me hardest is to hear his name read in church – even now, it still sounds intimately raw, and wrong.'

The memories that make this book, the images that are freshly painted onto the page, the tenderness, the honesty, the willingness to issue truth is a tribute to everyone who lived in that house in the fields near Eglish. Much better than any myth or legend, much better than the canonisation of a fine man and a brilliant footballer, this book is authentic and deeply moving. No finer tribute could be paid by one brother to another than to render him in truth.

## The Mackeys

There is a thing that binds together people who play sport with each other that cannot be shaken by time. It is more than sharing a field, more than sharing a dressing-room. It is related, in part, to remembrance of a time in your life when you were young and fit and able for everything. The shadows cast on a life by the passage of years, by the inevitable struggles, by the things that go wrong, the failures, the disappointments, the frustrations do not darken the joy of that time as it recedes into the past. Instead, those shadows cast that joy in even starker relief.

When a team or a group of players and their opponents strike a chord unlike any other, the remembrance is all the more moving. In that group of players there is always one who comes to epitomise the inherent spirit more than the rest – from the great Limerick hurling team of the 1930s, Mick Mackey was the one. His team won four Munster titles in a row and played in four All-Ireland finals: they won two of those finals – 1934 and 1936 – and, of course, came again in 1940 to win a third. They also won five National Hurling League titles in a row.

Mick Mackey was the foundation of this success: an icon who was feted for his determination, his intelligence, his selflessness and his absolute dedication to the cause. His reputation was related to how he played the game – and he played it hard. Just as with Anthony Foley, Mackey's was an inherited hardness. His father, John – better known as Tyler Mackey – was the captain of the Limerick team that won the 1910 Munster championship. Tyler's style of play was euphemistically described in the newspapers as 'direct' and 'robust'. A noted referee of the period, Willie Walsh, described Tyler as being 'of impetuous nature'. Tyler himself said that the toughest man he ever played against was one

Jim Spud Murphy from the Barrs in Cork. Tyler said of Spud that he was 'never one to bother overmuch with rules' – and he didn't mean that statement as an insult.

In the case of Mick Mackey, his physical approach was coloured by the presence at wing forward of his brother, John. Brothers playing on the same team changes the usual dynamics. In this case, as in many others, it meant a lot more timber being broken. As Mick Mackey said: 'With us, it was hit one, hit two.'

His physical prowess should not, of course, diminish the hurling skill which Mackey possessed. One without the other would not have allowed him develop into the crowd favourite that he became. The fondness with which Mick Mackey is remembered is also related to the fact that he was renowned for playing with a certain humour. The brilliant Tipperary hurler, Tommy Doyle, recalled a tournament match between Ahane and his own Thurles Sarsfields down in Newport in 1947. He recalled how a huge crowd turned up to see a game that was billed as the unofficial Munster club final.

Such was the importance of the game that the local parish priest decided to throw in the ball. As was still the norm eight players from each team lined up in the middle of the field. As the priest stepped back to roll in the ball, Mick Mackey shouted out: 'Remember lads, this is not the real throw-in!' Several of the Thurles players stood back as Mackey swept up the ball and set off on a trademark solo run through the defence before shooting a point. Doyle knocked great amusement out of the trick.

It was this sort of thing that led Mackey to recall later: 'I suppose I was a cool class of customer. It was good crack.

Even if you were beaten, somebody would say something and you could laugh about it. Maybe [Christy] Ring didn't get the same fun out of it.'

Central to this was an unshakeable love of his game. He played as long as he could and when he finished playing he stayed in the game as a coach and an administrator. He actually played his last match in 1955 when – well into his forties – he stood in goals for his employers, the ESB, in an inter-firms match. It was reported in the press that he made a series of outstanding saves.

That same year he trained the Limerick team that won the 1955 Munster championship. It was an entirely unexpected success. Clare had entered the final as strong favourites. Dermot Kelly, one of the players on the Limerick team, recalled Mackey's input on the day, saying: 'He got up on a table and spoke to us like I have never heard anyone speak since. It was so moving we knew we had to win.'

As the years passed, the hurlers of the 1930s – the Limerick ones and the ones they played against – were brought together at occasional reunions and awards ceremonies and at golf outings. Increasingly, though, they met at funerals, as they buried the men whom they had played against. In 1975, when John Keane, the great Waterford centre-back who regularly marked Mick Mackey, knew he was dying, he set off for Kilkenny and stayed the night with the great Jim Langton, another star of the 1930s. He went then to Cork to hurlers he had played against and on to Tralee where the old Limerick hurler, Jackie Power was living. The following day he set off for Limerick to meet Mick Mackey. He died on the way.

Just a few years later, Mick Mackey, indestructible in his prime, also died. On the day in September 1982 that he was buried in Castleconnell, a minute's silence was held at the Markets Field in Limerick when Limerick United were playing the Dutch side Alkmaar in the European Cup. Around the soccer field, all flags were flown at half-mast, just as they were across the county of Limerick. Five of Mackey's teammates from the great Limerick teams of the 1930s, including his brother John, were at the funeral. The rest had already passed on.

The men from Christy Ring's club – Glen Rovers – arrived in a mini-bus. Ring had himself already died, but out from the minibus stepped men such as Fox Collins who had played in the 1931 All-Ireland final. Men who had played against Mackey from Kilkenny, Tipperary, Waterford, Clare, Galway, Dublin and beyond travelled to the funeral. There were representatives from the government, the President and the army.

The chief concelebrant at the funeral mass was Fr Liam Kelly, whose father had played with Mackey and who had himself won a county championship with Ahane in 1955. Fr Kelly remembered what it was like to grow up in a parish where Mick Mackey was a god.

Quoting from Yeats, he noted that Mackey's was one of 'the names that stopped our childhood play'. He finished his sermon with a call to bring the past into the future: 'The dedication and self-sacrifice of Mick Mackey and his men is now folklore and can still serve as an inspiration to us all … Are we going to continue pursuing a comfortable and easy life? When we are in doubt do we just do nothing?

Do we ask what everyone else is doing before committing ourselves? ... If you are inclined to settle for a colourless, selfish conservatism, remember Mick Mackey. He tells us what human beings were made for and are capable of.'

## The Hurley Maker's Son

Larry Deeley was cutting ash trees to make hurleys when he died. It was the end of September 1978. He was felling the final tree of a day's work in a forest near Athlone when the upper part lurched and hit him on the temple. He collapsed bleeding into the sawdust on the ground. Two of his sons were working with him. They ran for help. The owner of the wood sought to revive him, but couldn't.

For forty years, Larry Deeley had cut down trees: the work was dangerous but his death came as a profound shock.

This shock – and the depth of grief that flowed around it – opens Patrick Deeley's book, *The Hurley Maker's Son*. It is a magnificent book. The book is a memoir of Patrick's life growing up as the son of a hurley-maker in the old hurling area of Tynagh in East Galway. This was a place where hurling was utterly embedded in the rhythms of life. It says much for the importance of hurling in East Galway that it was one of those few areas where the game continued to be played in the decades between the Famine and the founding of the GAA in 1884.

In 1966 – when Patrick was thirteen – Tynagh made it back to the Galway senior hurling final. They hadn't won it since the 1930s and defeat in that 1966 final proved a bitter pill to swallow. But the memories of that match remain vivid. This was a day of dust rising in the square as hurleys flew, a day when Paddy Fahy wiped 'a swathe of blood from his forehead casually as another man might discard his cap', a day when love of hurling as a spectacle was sealed.

Patrick, himself, played away all through his childhood – hurling games with his brothers descending into frequent rows, games with the neighbours and then, of course, games with the school and with underage teams in his club. There is much of this that will be familiar to anyone who has grown up in a hurling area or a hurling house – that feeling of holding a hurley for the first time is beautifully described and so are the moments of broken windows and muddied whitewashed walls.

But there was a crucial difference in this instance: he was a hurley maker's son. This brought a different meaning to hurleys, a different way of looking at them and ultimately a different understanding of what they were. The hurley-making process was lovingly tended by his father and the commitment to producing hurleys that were of the very highest mark is obvious to see.

The sawmill dominated the small farm and was central to its life.

Nonetheless, it is difficult to feel nostalgic for that world – there were too many flaws, too much pain for that to be the case. The struggle to make ends meet on a small farm, with a timber business where the margins were exceedingly narrow, was unrelenting. It was a struggle that was not helped by the failure of clubs to pay for the hurleys they had ordered or by the inevitable accidents that came along.

Then there is the context of that struggle: rural Ireland from the 1950s to the 1970s. Patrick loved his parents and respected them and understands everything that they did for him. Yet displays of fondness were in short supply: 'I scarcely recall a single kiss or hug between any of us.' For some children such absences may have been irrelevant – but for Patrick it was an absence that was keenly felt. In this, of course, as he freely admits, he was very much the product of the times, because 'such things just weren't done'.

But this is not a sort of *Angela's Ashes* for East Galway – there is too much joy in the book, and an absence of self-pity, for that to be the case. Instead, it recreates an era in a way that is unsentimental and respectful and honest: anyone who grew up in a rural area or in a small town will recognise parts of their own lives in the book.

This really matters – he may be the hurley maker's son, but the book is about much more than hurling. There is, for example, the stories of that great playground for children that is the family farm with its endless capacity for games of hide-and-seek and for climbing trees. The phrases heard when growing up stayed lodged in the mind: Uncle Mattie who dismissed a neighbour as someone who would 'begrudge piss its steam'.

And then into adolescence and just waiting, waiting, waiting for things to happen.

It may have appeared for that child that this was a world that would never end and that his parents 'both would always be there'. But it did end – and when Deeley writes of how he is perceived differently – and feels differently – when he returns home after moving away to the city, it is something that will be immediately recognised by anyone who has moved from home to a different area.

This is what makes *The Hurley Maker's Son* so special: like the very best books, it creates an atmosphere that is entirely unique – an atmosphere that never really leaves you. The book ends almost where it began, a few short weeks before his father's fatal accident. Patrick walks out to the field behind the sawmill to say good-bye and father and son simply say to each other: 'Mind yourself.' As he writes so painfully at the end: 'These are the last words that pass between them, but the boy will talk to the father for the rest of his life, and the father, though dead and gone, will talk to him.'

# 11 IDENTITY

Sports organisations depend on the clarity of their rules. Modern sport, with its extraordinary network of clubs and organisations, holds precise regulations for almost everything. From the meaning of membership to boundaries of play, rules shape everything. These rules are not, of course, immutable. They change all the time, reframed to respond to the ways sports change as people seek to find new ways to win. They change, also, when legislators seek to ensure that a game is played in a certain way. Usually, these are changes that are designed, in team games, to make play faster, more open, more skilful and – supposedly by extension – more attractive to spectators, as well as to players.

But it is one thing for rulemakers to seek to legislate for how a game should be played, and altogether another to legislate for matters of identity. When it comes to matters of sport and identity, it is immediately apparent the extent to which sport reflects society. Most of the time, sporting organisations reveal a deeply conservative, almost reactionary approach. Sport was – and remains – run through with perceptions of what it means to play a particular game, about what sporting preferences say about an individual.

The questions keep coming: how is a person's identity bound up with how they carry themselves when they play sport? How does the desire to compete and to win trump everything else? What are the things that men and women are willing to trade in pursuit of their sporting ambitions? The answers to these questions are unending.

Watching sport grappling with issues of identity offers a window on social and cultural change, locally and across the world; this extends back into history and is profoundly affected by this history. Much of the organisation of international sport is based on the nation-state. But the realities of migration, of deep-running conflicts about where a line should run on a map, and of the enduring impact of colonialism repeatedly undermine attempts to produce a clear set of acceptable sporting rules which map identity onto teams that represent a nation-state. Further, the triumph of capitalism, the commercialisation of sport, the wish for a state and its sporting organisations to win glory, and the desire of people to make money by forging a professional career in sport has also undermined clarity. But it is in its approach to gender that the difficulties which sporting bodies have in engaging with identity is most obviously revealed.

## Perfume and Embrocation

In sport, the past holds a tight rein on the present and, when it comes to the relationship between gender and identity, the sporting mould shaped by the Victorian world has never properly been broken. Almost every national and international organisation which now governs sport was founded in the years between 1850 and 1900. These institutions reflected the gender prejudices of the times in which they were formed. This was – emphatically – a man's world and sport inevitably reflected this simple fact. But the newly formed sporting organisations such as the Football Association (1863) and the Rugby Football Union (1871) were not just set up for men, but for a very definite type of man. The sporting male was to be strong, vigorous and tough. At least that it is how the rhetoric of the time presented it. This was a rhetoric that was pulled from the elite public schools of England (all, essentially, the preserve of boys of a certain class) and ultimately applied to the developing world of sport. The rules made by these organisations were passed around the British empire and the story told was that boys were made into men by playing by these rules. Indeed, sport was perceived as the perfect academy to learn the skills that made life possible – provided you were male.

In this world, sport was to be restricted to men; indeed, to be good at sport was to be naturally male. A journalist writing for *Sport*, a weekly Irish sportspaper, noted in the 1880s that playing organised sport was crucial to discourage effeminacy in an age of 'gentleman's corsets' and men writing 'maudlin poems in praise of each other'.

There was a place for women in this world – but that place was not on the playing field. Women were expected to watch and admire, present the garlands afterwards, swoon, and help with the catering. There was also a certain pride expressed in this discrimination. The Yorkshire Rugby Union was told by one of its officers in 1889: 'We have no dealings with women here.' This point was repeatedly reinforced. For example, forty years later in 1932, a one-time president of the Rugby Football Union said: 'Ours is a game not founded for women.'

Among many women, too, there was a lack of conviction regarding their own suitability for athletic endeavour. Wealthy women, who might have been expected to lead a sporting movement for women, held other priorities. It was considered vulgar in the late nineteenth century to have a robust fitness. This very abstinence from activity made women inevitably more prone to illness. And the less women did, the less they appeared able to do. Fighting against prejudice is made all the more difficult when it is wrapped in some pseudo-intellectual justification. Science fed the belief that men and women were complementary opposites. Basically, it was still held by many that excessive sporting activity could diminish a woman's capacity to have children. Women were considered only to have a fixed amount of energy and wasting it on sporting activity deflected them from fulfilling the roles of wife and mother.

Sporting discrimination against women was not something that was the preserve of the United Kingdom. The visionaries of continental European sport believed that women had no place in their world of sport. The founder of the modern Olympic Games, Baron Pierre de Coubertin, wrote in the 1890s that women's sport was 'against the laws of nature', and that 'the eternal role of woman in this world was to be a companion of the male and mother of the family, and she should be educated towards those functions'.

In time – but only slowly – the boundaries began to shift. This shift reflected the changing place of women in society.

Independent women sought their own place in the world, working in the civil service, graduating from universities, living on their own. Sport played a significant part in shifting the perceptions of what a woman was capable of doing. That women began to redefine sport for themselves is a tribute to the pioneering few who defied the conventions of their age. They established their own organisations for golf and camogie, for example, and women's tennis became hugely popular.

But there was no playing place for women in rugby or soccer or in the GAA. Basically, across the modern sporting world there were games considered to be suitable for women and games that were equally considered unsuitable. In the late nineteenth century, the response of sporting women was to create an alternative sporting culture around lacrosse and netball. In this culture, women sought competitive sport by working around the prejudices of their age and constructing their own sporting world. This changed only exceptionally slowly in the twentieth century and every advance was tempered by a residual tendency to patronise and to parody the sporting female. Indeed, women's sport has routinely been belittled, trivialised, or simply ignored. There is no denying this essential truth. Over time, the overt discrimination of Victorian times has largely disappeared, but its remnants have determined that sportswomen have remained very much the poor relation to men.

The last fifty years has seen sports previously the preserve of men open up to women. This was a reflection on changes in wider society and on the place of sport within that society. An example of this is the development of women's Gaelic football. The *Evening Press* began its report on what it described as the first ever intercounty ladies' football match, played in Tullamore, Co. Offaly on Sunday, 29 July 1973, noting that 'perfume took over from embrocation as the prevailing odour in the dressingrooms yesterday when Offaly hosted Kerry'. The journalist who wrote the report of the match noted that the game had initially been seen as a bit of a joke and that there were some diehards and other freestyle sneers who had turned up just to mock the idea of women attempting to play Gaelic football. The reporter performed a neat pivot in the article, however. He claimed that by the end of the game those same sneers had been converted: 'Two dedicated teams quickly earned their admiration, and some of the combined movements proved that these girls have little to learn from their male counterparts.'

The game in Tullamore confirmed the momentum that was clearly gathering around women's endeavours to play organised Gaelic football. There had been some games started in the 1920s but it was only during the 1960s that women had begun to organise themselves into teams – and then into clubs – in counties such as Offaly, Waterford and Tipperary. Initially, those games were played almost always as seven-a-side matches organised in conjunction with local carnivals and festivals around the country. From this tentative beginning, by the early 1970s the game had evolved to the establishment of leagues and then local championships in Cork, Waterford and Tipperary. The next logical step was the establishment of an association for women's football. When that did happen, the symbolism of the moment was stark.

On Thursday evening, 18 July 1974 a small group of men and women gathered in Hayes' Hotel in Thurles, Co. Tipperary. Fully ninety years had passed since the Gaelic Athletic Association had been founded under the same roof. When Michael Cusack and Maurice Davin had founded the GAA in 1884, they had pledged to open its doors to men of all classes and to give men something to look forward to rather than 'an everlasting round of labour'. It never seems to have occurred to them that women, too, might wish to play hurling or Gaelic football. Anyway, the upshot of the 1974 meeting was the establishment of the Ladies' Gaelic Football Association.

Over the subsequent decades, that association has entirely revolutionised the way in which women played Gaelic games. Firstly, the rules of Gaelic football were modified to allow for the ball to be picked off the ground and to restrict the level of physical contact. An All-Ireland championship was established and women's football was extended across every county in Ireland. Through the 1970s and 1980s, the association developed its championship and league structures, established underage structures and improved coaching. Allowing for this, women playing Gaelic football was simply not accorded the respect or progression that was merited. It was not until the 1990s that significant growth was experienced and women's Gaelic football grew at an extraordinary rate. This growth was characterised by the success in developing the intercounty level of the game in tandem with a huge surge in grassroots participation. The reasons for the growth were several and largely straightforward. Financial investment allied with the simple fact of working hard, putting bodies on the ground, and coaching in clubs and in schools, began to reap dividends and the games developed in areas of the country where they had not previously been played.

Women's rugby was even slower to get established in Ireland. Here's a simple comparison: the first international national rugby match involving Irish men was played in 1875, while the first international rugby match involving Irish women was played in 1993. That sentence, in the baldness of its detail, reveals an ocean of chauvinism, ignorance, neglect and denial. It was Scotland who provided the first opposition in 1993 and the match was played in Edinburgh on St Valentine's Day – it ended in a 10–0 loss. More importantly, that year also saw the establishment of the Irish Women's Rugby Football Union. That union was borne of an alliance between ten teams of women who had begun to play rugby from the early 1980s.

During that decade, women's rugby matches were played on an ad-hoc basis by a growing number of women who – by the end of the 1980s – numbered some 200. This led, in turn, to the establishment of the All-Ireland Rugby League in November 1992 with teams drawn from as far apart as Belfast, Dublin and Limerick. The final of that first league was played at Donnybrook and drew some 1,500 to see Blackrock defeat UCD. Central to the early success of the league was the commitment of their sponsors Standard Life Assurance Company who brought invaluable profile to the endeavour.

It is a simple fact that women's rugby was not supported properly by the existing men's teams. It is true that Blackrock

Rugby Club brought the women's team into their structure, provided training facilities and expertise, and gave their grounds for matches. But most clubs simply ignored what was happening. As Mary O'Beirne, the president of the new Irish Women's Rugby Football Union pointed out at the time, this was extremely shortsighted: 'If more Irish rugby clubs were to become involved with women's rugby, I feel it would be to the clubs' advantage and widen the scope of the game.' There are plenty of rugby clubs in Ireland who have yet to fully embrace that lesson. The same applies to rugby clubs around the world.

## At Grass

There is only one certainty in every sporting career – it will end.

When that end comes, the sporting world will spin on regardless of who or what has been lost. For all the montage of memories, the story of sport will shift on so quickly that even the immediate past will seem more like ancient history. Or even mythology.

It is with horses, rather than with humans, that the poet Philip Larkin beautifully revealed this truth.

In his poem, 'At Grass', Larkin wrote of two horses in a meadow, sheltering in the shade, one wandering about eating grass while the other looks on. The ageing horses were anonymous by then, but that had not always been the case. Some fifteen years previously, some two dozen races had brought them fame:

'To fable them: faint afternoons
Of Cups and Stakes and Handicaps.'

They mattered so much in their day, in the pomp of their
greatness, that thousands and thousands of people came to
see them run – and win. Their successes were such that their
names would live on forever in almanacs.

The imagery of those days – the rows of empty cars
surrounding a racetrack, the litter lying on the grass, the
silk of the jockeys, the dash of the horses – extends across
the history of modern horse racing. Larkin's two horses are
part of that history, champions who were once celebrated,
once had their names etched onto trophies, once were truly
relevant in the unfolding of the endlessly busy, endlessly
rejuvenating world of sport.

In the poem, however, time has pushed on and the
horses race no longer. They are the stuff of anecdote and
remembrance – but they do not matter anymore to the
sporting contest, at least not really. Their (sporting) day is
done.

There is a question in the middle of the poem that sits
right at the heart of the life of those who finish up in sport.
It reads:

'Do memories plague their ears like flies?'

That notion of the plague of memories filling a head,
crowding out the present with an insistent press of noiseless
imagery, is what does the most damage to a post-play
life. How do you live forwards when your life pulls you
backwards into its past, time and again? It is one thing if
everybody else pulls you back into it with questions and

stories, but another when you do it to yourself, unable to let go of faded glories.

Larkin notes how, for the horses, there were years of 'starting gates, the crowd and cries', all of which pulled them away from the meadows. The upshot of this was 'Summer by summer all stole away.'

This is a question for everyone who dedicates so much of their lives – more accurately, so many of those years when they are in their prime – to the pursuit of sporting excellence.

Do you think, looking back, that it was really worth it? Were all the sacrifices worthwhile? Was what was given up merited? Was stealing away summer after summer from yourself really something that makes sense, a decision that stands the test of time? Crucially, was enough fun taken out of the journey, or was the obsession with the result overpowering of all else?

As the poem ends, Larkin sees that the horses are standing at ease in a meadow. They gallop now for what must be joy, without anybody straining to watch them in field-glasses or putting their galloping to a stopwatch. Nobody comes to look at them, except those who care for them.

Best of all, out in this sheltered scene, away from everything, they have 'slipped their names'.

It is one thing for two horses to slip their names, though, but altogether another for a human being. The very human emotions of nostalgia and regret cannot be shaken off in the manner of Larkin's horses who shake their heads in the contentment of a summer meadow filled with grass and stripped of obligation.

Perhaps, ultimately, the nub of the matter comes down to a matter of identity. It is unknowable the extent to which a horse may or may not be shaped by the prime of their sporting endeavours. But for many competitors, sport is such an obsession, so central to everything that they have sought and thought throughout their days, that it comes to colonise their identity.

How do you learn to live without the thing that has become so much a part of what you are, the thing that you most likely love doing more than anything else?

It is certainly the case that there are those who are able to simply move on immediately. They walk out of the dressing-room door for a last time, knowing they are done, and there is scarcely a glimpse backwards. There is a wonderful word in Irish – *riastradh* – that relates to how Cú Chulainn, in the middle of a battle, managed to shape-shift, or to contort himself, to face new struggles.

For others, the adjustment to a life after sport proves relatively straightforward over time. They refocus on other aspects of their life, conscious of the hole that has been left, perhaps occasionally wistful of what has been lost never to be regained, but broadly comfortable in accepting the passage of the years and the diminution of their physical capabilities.

There are those who never really get over what they once were and are unable to cope properly with a new dawn whose arrival is unwelcome and whose inevitability was known but resisted. This is manifest in every sport and is played out in the mental and physical turmoil of the individuals who are caught up in its misery.

Life after sport is something that ignores all boundaries – for example, it transcends gender and is oblivious to whether someone was an amateur or a professional. No amount of money or medals saves you from the end.

Philip Larkin got the idea for his poem when he slipped away from work to the cinema one afternoon in the first week of January 1950. Before the main feature started, a short film depicting the life of an old racehorse, Brown Jack, stuck with him. Brown Jack had been famous before the war, but now – in a sort of 'Where is Brown Jack now?' piece – he was portrayed in a field without jockey or harness, cropping the grass and galloping freely. It is claimed that the vista created by Larkin was one of contentment at the end of a well-lived life.

It may be that the poem can indeed be read as a sort of admiration for such a life, but its deep melancholy is difficult to escape. Because, like Philip Larkin's horses, for every sportsperson there is no happy alternative to living out years (even decades) 'at grass', however contented they may be. Nothing beats playing – and nothing can replace it. As Larkin concluded:

> 'Only the groom, and the groom's boy,
> With bridles in the evening come.'

## The Pursuit of Success

Ethical issues around sport usually revolve around the pursuit of success. But when do we ever discuss the meaning of success? When it comes down to it, debate around the idea of winning by whatever means necessary is something that flares into sight, only at the time of controversy, and rarely in a reasoned way.

The capacity of people to excite themselves is particularly acute at those very moments when their team has been the victim of an injustice. On a national level there is the Thierry Henry handball; on a provincial rugby level there is the remembrance of how Neil Back, the Leicester forward, brazenly broke the rules at a scrum and denied Munster the opportunity to win what would then have been their first Heineken Rugby Cup in 2002. But it was Neil Back who got to the nub of the matter when he was interviewed afterwards. His pithy response was: 'I did what I had to do to win the game.'

The outrage that followed was understandable on one level but its credibility is somewhat undercut by the fact that if Neil Back had been wearing a Munster jersey he would most likely have been made a Freeman of Limerick and celebrated for his native guile. When it comes down to it, sleights of hand (or acts of random violence) which benefit our own teams are either indulged, excused, or willingly accepted as fortune finally shining on the downtrodden who have been too long oppressed but are now standing up for themselves.

The greater point here is that, generally, controversies occur around particular incidents and are driven by that incident. These incidents always obscure any possible debate around the purpose of sport. This too is entirely understandable – when it comes down to it, there is nothing quite as entertaining as a good controversy.

Indeed, central to any understanding of the importance of sport in the modern world is understanding the attraction of controversy – especially when it is absolutely absurd. Witness Roy Keane, Mick McCarthy and Saipan in the days before the 2002 World Cup final. What ensued was an extraordinary spectacle as the public, politicians, and the media convulsed on one side or the other. Sane and sensible people said and wrote extreme things as they recast the dispute as a battle between a 'new' Ireland, unready to accept second-best, out now to beat the world at soccer, especially since we have redefined global economics through the Celtic Tiger; and an 'old' Ireland, happy merely to be asked along at all to the party, and sure if we have to stand in the corner that's grand too.

Those who sought to portray the event as some sort of Greek tragedy seemed actually to believe what they were claiming. Or did they? How much was sincerely felt, and how much were people simply revelling in the great absurdity of it all? It was as if having already experienced the pleasures of attending two World Cups, the Irish needed now to find a new passion to make the competition worth the bother. In the process, they once more revealed the national talent for hysteria and melodrama.

But that insistent question remains – what do you win for? There are any number of answers that can be offered here, each of which is peculiar unto the individual. Is it glory, or fame, or personal satisfaction, or pride? Do you win for your family, your community, your country – or just for yourself? Do you win for money? I want to turn to this last question next – this relationship between amateurism and professionalism. The words amateur and professional are bandied about by players and managers and supporters and journalists – and in this bandying they are used in ways that seem to me to be entirely flawed.

For example, a man through on goal in a GAA match is pulled down and someone will describe it as a professional foul. A favoured team runs through a less fancied opposition and is described as doing a professional job. On the other side of the coin, when a professional sportsperson does something poorly it can be described as amateur hour or amateurish, or in failing to commit a cynical act in pursuit of victory is condemned for not doing the professional thing.

The use of these words is something of a reflex response, but this matters because it is a reflex that epitomises a common misunderstanding of just how badly amateurs wish to win. After all, a professional will ordinarily be paid whether he or she wins or loses, albeit they might be paid less in defeat than in victory. But medals are the wages of amateur sport and to deny the desire of the amateur to win – and ignore the willingness of the amateur to do what is necessary to win – is to ignore the competitive spirits and instincts that are readily apparent.

Are women more ethical in sport than men? History provides no evidence that women are markedly different to men when it comes to sport. I temper that by saying that our modern sporting world – created largely during the last decades of the nineteenth century – was (to put it at its mildest) an unwelcoming place for women. The Victorian press was filled with jokes about women and their hockey legs or their incapacity to play. One Irish paper laughed:

'When a woman throws a brickbat, the great problem seems to be not how to hit the target, but how she can avoid knocking her brains out with her elbow.'

Notwithstanding that, women have demonstrated a capacity for conduct which echoes that of the sporting male. Look at violence, for example. The sheriff of Kildare reported from 1782 of a football match near the Curragh. The report noted how a fight after the match between the two teams had drawn in spectators. During the fight, one man was 'brought to the ground by the stroke of a bottle from the wife of a person whom he had just knocked down; and the woman's feelings for her husband being stimulated by liquor, she cut the head of his opponent to innumerable pieces, and immediately received from one of the combatants a casual blow that fractured her own. There is little prospect of her recovery.'

Or, more recently, what about the drugtaking of women athletes such as Florence Griffith-Joyner or Marion Jones? What about the generations of female gymnastics coaches whose sweatshops reduce young girls to performing battery hens, in search of Olympic gold? For every overbearing father such as Earl Woods who produces a Tiger Woods as a sort of parenting project in constructing an elite athlete, there are overbearing mothers such as Betty Chang whose son Michael, a brilliant tennis player, won the French Open at seventeen.

Consider, more locally, the antics of parents at sporting venues all over this country – every day there are children who are being embarrassed and much, much worse by their parents, as they seek to live their lives vicariously through their children and in the process pretty much ensure that such living is impossible.

Where do modern sporting clubs and governing bodies sit in all of this? The connections that people make in sport can sustain them through life: for some people sport is what makes school bearable and work possible. But the usage of sports clubs is not inherently benign: sports clubs can be bastions of privilege and can further age-old prejudices.

In sports clubs – and in their governing bodies, nationally and internationally – there are many, many extraordinary people who dedicate themselves to improving the lives of others through sport. They are beacons of all that is good in modern life. But there are also others who do not merit that description. The megalomania of certain sports administrators is apparent for all to see. In terms of soccer, for example, you don't need to cast your eyes as high as Gianni Infantino to see the evidence for that – indeed, you don't even have to leave the island.

The packaging of modern sport allows people to imagine that the modern sporting world – for good or ill – is entirely different to that which has gone before. But at its core, it is not so. Instead, modern sport is about people finding new ways to doing the same thing. When it comes to ethics – just as with every aspect of sport – there are no golden ages, no time where we can look back into history and say: there is our benchmark, our ethical nirvana.

# 12 AMERICA

Some of the very best episodes of *The Simpsons* are centred on sport. That means some of Homer's finest lines are sporting ones. There is none finer than his 'But this might be my last chance to win one!', issued after he was caught trying to steal the Super Bowl trophy in 1999. The attempted theft took place when Homer headed in a bus with other men from Springfield to Miami for the Super Bowl. Having made their way into the stadium – overcoming the problem of having originally bought counterfeit tickets – they see no football and even miss the half-time show. But as if to underline the meaning of the day, they feast on burgers and chicken drumsticks and guzzle bottles of beer with a certain heroism. It is not just American football that features in *The Simpsons*, but also boxing, baseball, ice hockey, golf and tennis. And always Homer's insights into sport are epic. He tells his daughter when she plays ice hockey: 'Lisa, if the Bible has taught us nothing else, and it hasn't, it's that girls should stick to girls' sports, such as hot-oil wrestling, foxy boxing and such-and-such ...' His advice to his son on the value of taking part in a mini-golf tournament is clear: 'Come on, Bart! Remember what Vince

Lombardi said: "If you lose, you're out of the family!"'

That *The Simpsons* is a parody of American culture and society, its media and celebrity obsession, and ultimately of the way people think and behave in general, means that it could never have been made without episodes on sport. It has run for more than thirty seasons, beginning in 1989, and the centrality of sport to American society during these years is undeniable: Middle America without the vast commercialised behemoths of football, basketball, ice hockey and baseball is unrecognisable. It is not just the playing of the sports, but the manner in which they have colonised so much of American popular culture that matters. Throughout the lifetime of *The Simpsons*, the Super Bowl was ordinarily the most-watched television programme of the year. But it had also been refashioned to appeal even to those who had no interest in American football. The half-time shows, and the discourse around the cost of buying advertisement space in the course of the game, gathered an importance that lived outside the sport. All of this is in that 1999 Super Bowl episode when Homer tried to steal the trophy, and it can be reduced to one word, when he stands in the stadium in Miami, on the cusp of actually seeing the game, throws his two arms in the air and exclaims: 'Football!'

## Fenway Park

It's hard not to eat your way through a baseball match. When you walk into the ground there's the hotdogs and the fries. That smell of frying onions is a timeless magnet to anyone who has had the benefit of a couple of pints. But the game is about to start and the queue is hefty so it's straight to the seats in a tremendous show of discipline.

Of course, that's only posture. The first break in the play comes after a couple of minutes and the smell of the onions has done its harm so it's back down the steps and into the queue. When you get to the top and the food is ordered, it seems sensible to throw in another beer as well. No point in queueing twice. Back up to the seat with a big tray and settle in for the evening.

The stadium is gorgeous – Fenway Park in Boston, the oldest baseball park in the big leagues. It's a lovely warm night after a lovely hot day and the sun is only now dying behind the stands. The crowd in the grandstand are moving in and out, greeting each other, sitting down, standing up, and dancing.

The dancing comes as a bit of a surprise. Breaks in the play are filled with tunes that draw people to their feet. There's music from the Clash and the Rolling Stones and Justin Bieber. The best of the dancers are drawn from the Harvard University graduation class in the rows just in front. They have come to the game to mark the end and the beginning. And they're drinking and eating and dancing (all at the same time) and just in great form.

The challenge to discipline continues: young men are walking up and down the aisles selling monster bags of popcorn and large trays filled with big cartons of lemonade. It's hard to look away from them – and hard also to look away from the other men who are selling ice cream. More ballast.

It's not right to say that the game isn't being watched.

It is, for sure, it's just that the action happens in slivers and passing the time in between is pleasure in itself. All the while, the hum of chat rises from the stands, broken by the occasional cheering and groaning. The biggest cheer comes when the star hitter, David Ortiz, steps up and swings at a pitch. Ortiz is beloved of the Red Sox fans (his name being bandied around during the steroid scandals that rocked baseball has now been long forgotten). The statistics show that he is one of the greatest players ever to play for the club – but he is by now forty and his athleticism is much diminished. He still has power, but it is fading and this is his farewell season.

Every night now that he plays in Fenway Park seems to be touched with emotion. In truth, Ortiz hasn't been in great form of late but tonight – on this play – he connects with the ball and sends it down low to the left corner of the field. The crowd scream and shout with delight, all around people are on their feet. The fun in this sequence of play is only starting, however: Ortiz can't shift through the gears anymore and it feels certain that he would have been happy to amble to first base, given any sort of a fair wind.

The problem is that the Boston Red Sox are losing pretty heavily and if the game is to be saved, he needs to do something a little more. So Ortiz sets off on a sprint, gets around first base and heads for second. It's going to be a close run thing, as the fielders are zipping the ball across the field and it looks likely to reach second base before Ortiz does – meaning that he will be out. In a desperate late act at salvaging the situation, Ortiz dives and slides. It's a fractional call, but the umpire signals that he has made it. The crowd erupts, but a TV review is called. While the footage is being played and replayed, Ortiz is gathering himself on the field, getting his breath back and chatting to the fielders around him. After the review, the decision stands and Ortiz is safe. The crowd go wild – it's the biggest cheer of the night.

Someone starts the Mexican wave. Actually, two lads start the Mexican wave. They're well into their forties – old enough to know better. It's hard to know why it doesn't really take off, maybe it's because jumping out of a seat is not always easy when you're this full.

Despite all the drink, only one man appears to be properly goosed. He walks up the steps looking like he's wrestling with the Invisible Man. He's talking away to nobody in particular. He sits into a seat. And then moves. Tries another seat. Gets up. And then pours himself back down the steps. His business is more easily completed under the stand than in it. The joke about Fenway Park being the best bar in Boston is easily understood.

The game began at 7.10pm; it's now nearly 10pm. A new hunger has set in – not the type of hunger that means you need food, more that you just actually miss eating.

The good news is that, out the back, more men are selling more food. A band is playing out through the window of a bar and people are inside dancing and singing.

In Fenway Park, the game is still continuing – even though it's really over. The Red Sox have been poor tonight and are being soundly beaten by the Baltimore Orioles. The two teams were level at the top of the table before tonight, but the Orioles have been so much better from start to finish that it is difficult to see the season playing out well for

Boston. Despite the loss, the fans heading off into the night are devoid of rancour – the length of the season (Boston will play some 160 games in around 180 days) means that sustained vitriol at losing would turn Fenway Park into an epic, interminable episode of *Liveline*. The place is too good for that – and so is the game itself. And anyway, the Boston Red Sox are playing again tomorrow – time to meet the challenge again.

## Lunchtime

The white man in the suit was sweating. The jacket was off, the tie was loose and the sleeves were rolled up. It was hot – not the brutal, sweltering heat of the hottest summer days in New York – but hot nonetheless. Overhead, the trees were swaying gently to the breeze. The dance of the leaves meant the spots of sunlight that hit the table moved, and moved again. It wasn't the sun that was making the man sweat, though – it was the game.

He was immersed in a lunchtime game of table tennis, well into his forties and struggling to cope with the precision of his opponent. That opponent – a tall black man wearing cycling shorts and with long dreadlocks bouncing off his back – was smiling and bouncing, clearly loving the contest. And the standard was decent – but only decent, not outrageous. These were ordinary players having a bash.

Time and again, the man in the suit went for a big, top-spinning forehand to end the rally with a glorious flourish; he kept missing. He swung hard and hit the ball well, but he was off by a foot or more every single time. He talked to himself after every miss, mouthed the occasional expletive to himself, and slow-motioned the type of swing he wished to make.

In the next rally, he missed again.

In play after play, the guy in the dreadlocks just kept hitting percentages, kept putting the ball back over the net and then, when he was ready, set his opponent up to let him have his big swing. When the miss came, he smiled in sympathy, and said 'Great hit, man!' Then he served again.

Finally, one of the big forehands dipped and spun and clipped the end of the table, before flying off across the pathway. The crowd who had gathered to watch cheered and the man in the suit punched the air. It was a small but lovely victory earned against a wider defeat.

A few years earlier when the tables first opened, a sign on the side offered gentle instruction on how to react to results: 'You are welcome to be polite, considerate and courteous in victory and defeat.' There was no doubting that here. When the game ended, the men shook hands in the way that modern men in cities do – a sort of clasp of hands, followed by a shoulder bump.

Almost immediately, the next game started between two players who had waited patiently for their turn – just as those behind them in the queue were also waiting for their own hit.

The two table-tennis tables sit on the edge of Bryant Park, a space about the size of a soccer pitch, not far from Times Square in the middle of New York. All around Bryant Park people are eating sandwiches and hotdogs and burgers – and drinking coffee and sparkling water and red wine. There are people playing chess and two men are trying to juggle. Over the far side, there is a putting green and the square is also used for the French game of boules. A carousel remakes the music and motion of childhood.

The table tennis is a recent addition to the park, which is more than 130 years old. Now every day, table-tennis matches take place in ten-minute slots. The bats and the balls are provided free of charge. For those who are inspired to compete, monthly singles, doubles and mixed doubles competitions are organised (with elite or ranked players banned from playing) in the evenings from May to October. Companies hire them out for team-building evenings – the surrounding stalls and restaurants surely oil those outings.

For decades the park was run down and infamous as a site of multiple muggings and drug deals. By the 1970s it was avoided by any discerning locals, before a decade-long regeneration project transformed it into a place where people pour into, before, during and after their working day in the surrounding office blocks. The people who run Bryant Park claim (with a mixture of pride and hubris) that it is 'the greatest public space in the world'. Whatever about that, there can be no denying that they succeed in their mission to make the park something special in the life of the city.

There are two things of particular interest here. The first is that the park is run by a private company who act as agents for the city government. The Bryant Park Corporation was founded in 1980 and manages everything in the park, from the toilets and the gardens, to the table-tennis tables and the chessboards.

What they put on is put on for free. It is essentially made possible by raising money through sponsorship. From Google to Citibank, and from the New York Times to Evian, the ability of the Bryant Park Corporation to raise money to develop – and redevelop – their space is hugely impressive.

The upshot is that a park which was essentially lost to urban recreation now attracts up to six million people per year. The time-honoured policy of making a place safe by attracting people to it at all hours has been crucial – and table tennis has played its part in this.

Which brings us to the second point of interest. The Parks and Recreations Department in New York has been putting in table-tennis tables across the five boroughs of New York over the past decade. None of these other tables are in places that thrive quite as spectacularly as Bryant Park, but each serve their own function and are fitted to their own environment.

Putting the tables in cost relatively little money and has used up little space. Crucially, they give people a place to play together. Equally crucially – they are for people of all ages. More than that, when table tennis is played in public, it often serves to draw people to stop and watch – or at least to slow down as they pass.

## Irish-Americans

The poet Patrick Kavanagh only wrote a little about Gaelic football, but what he wrote was wonderful. He understood its place in rural Ireland and his observations on the language of the game and its rhythms were perfectly judged.

This was an understanding that extended beyond Ireland. In one article he told of how his brother told him a story of how, on a lovely Sunday morning, he was strolling around San Francisco on the edge of the Pacific Ocean when he saw 'men of a rural Irish complex' hurrying along with little bundles under their arms.

A short distance away, he came upon a Gaelic football match: 'Everything was at home: there were the men running up and down the unpailed sideline slicing at the toes which encroached with hurleys and crying: "Keep back there now, Keep back there now." All around the pitch, the familiar battlecrys of the Dalcassians were to be heard: "Gut yer man", "Bog into him." Not a man of them had ever left home and the mysterious Pacific was just a boghole, gurgling with eels and frogs.'

This arresting sight, the feelings it created and the thoughts it provoked were, to Patrick Kavanagh, 'something queer and wonderful'.

Kavanagh was writing back in 1950 when the stream of emigrants flowing out of Ireland had swelled to a huge tide of humanity. That tide flowed freely through the 1950s and when you go to America now, the imprint of that generation is readily apparent. It reshaped Irish emigrant communities that had been growing even before the Great Famine of the 1840s – those communities, of course, overflowed during and after that Famine, greening American cities for decade after decade. More recently, the surges of emigration through the 1980s and over the last decade have brought renewal to Irish-America.

The great sweep of the history of Irish emigration to

America can be seen through sport. This is true from the generations of Irish emigrants and their descendants who took to baseball and American football, for example. It can be seen in the Irish athletes who won Olympic medals in the colours of America (glorying in beating British athletes, in particular).

And it can be seen in the history of Gaelic games in American cities.

In Boston, Gaelic games are thriving, not least at the magnificent facilities in Canton, outside Boston city. But the games can be seen in the city itself, also. On a summer's afternoon, on Boston Common – a wonderful public space in the heart of city – two young Irish men pucked a ball back and forward to each other. They looked like students over on J1 visas for the summer and the city moved around them as they swung their hurleys. Hardly a word was spoken, just the ball flying over and back and over. It was, in its own way, utterly compelling – and it echoed a largely forgotten past.

In the early days of the GAA, in 1888, when a team of hurlers and athletes came over to raise money for the association at home and to establish the GAA in America by putting on exhibitions, it was to this very piece of land that they had come.

They had arrived in Boston to huge acclaim and a banquet was put on in their honour by Irish Americans. The banquet saw ward politicians compete with each other to pay homage to the visitors on the eve of their match.

The following day, Boston Common was thronged to see the GAA men compete in athletics events against local men – and also to see them put on an exhibition of hurling. That exhibition was – as the euphemism would have it – keenly contested: at least three players got properly injured as the city echoed to the sound of breaking timber.

That was not actually the first hurling that was played in Boston. In many significant Irish communities in the decades before the founding of the GAA, men had played hurling on green spaces in America. They had done this in New York in the 1780s and San Francisco in the 1860s, for example – and they also hurled in Boston.

During the 1870s and early 1880s, crowds of up to 6,000 people turned out to see hurling matches played by teams of Irishmen on parks and fields around Boston, as Paul Darby has written. The rules they played by had evolved sufficiently to include the use of referees and the game saw the players fill recognisable positions of play.

Among those who turned out to spectate were people drawn from the expansive working-class Irish enclaves of South Boston, but also families from the city's expanding Irish middle classes. Indeed, the local press reported that 'nearly all of the prominent Irish Americans in Boston and vicinity' attended to see a game that was so old that it 'takes us back into the remotest antiquity'.

They even played for the Boyle O'Reilly Cup – donated by the Fenian John Boyle O'Reilly, who had earlier escaped from penal servitude in Australia for revolutionary activities in the 1880s. A statue to Boyle O'Reilly stands in the Fenway in Boston and his support for hurling helped the game prosper until the establishment of the GAA in 1884. It should be said, however, that such were the disputes over the Boyle O'Reilly Cup that the Massachusetts courts were called on to adjudicate between the rival clubs in a series of lawsuits.

The hurlers of Boston adopted the GAA's rules for the game. In June 1886, what appears to be the first game of football played under the rules of the GAA in America was played on Boston Common between teams drawn from Kerry and Galway.

Looking back at those years from the vantage point of a new millennium, it is extraordinary how the organisation of hurling and Gaelic football has changed. On the streets of Boston, men, women and children wander around wearing the jerseys of their counties, or their clubs. On the T (the local tram system), young men and women travel to training, or to GAA meetings, talk of matches and of their lives in the city.

It is an expression of local identity and national identity given additional meaning in this international context. It is also a connection to home that transcends several centuries.

Hurling on Boston Common – and football along the sea in San Francisco: timeless rituals of pleasure and place.

# 13 BOOKS

'Every book, like every blackbird, is different,' wrote John Berger in his introduction to Timothy O'Grady's fictionalised memoir, *I Could Read The Sky*. In this book, an Irish emigrant in London, a man who left the west of Ireland to labour in England in the second half of the twentieth century, leaves both a historical document and a social record of his life. He finds himself alone at the end of that century, looking back across decades of a life lived between two islands. The full force of the conflict between dislocation and belonging that can afflict the emigrant is everywhere apparent. The way O'Grady uses music, the way he weaves it into the book from the very first page, is vital to the story. In the telling of his life, music becomes a focal point as a binding tie to home and a fundamental expression of emigrant traditions abroad. This is at once something absolutely intimate, something that draws him back into the world of his family, of the kitchen at home, of playing with his father. At the other end it is something that is public and collective and even universal. It is a magnificent, moving book – the memory of a man's life and through that memory the telling of the history of a people, of a way of life that has now essentially disappeared.

The role that music plays in O'Grady's book, its centrality to a life, is something that is akin to the role played by sport in so many other lives. This is something that is captured in the best of sporting autobiographies – although there are also many poor ones, formulaic in their determination not to reveal anything much of interest beyond superficial anecdote. The way sport runs through lives in so many different ways is captured not just in memoirs, but also in biographies, histories and in fiction. When that capturing is at its best, it brings you into that life and from that life out into the wider world. Breandán Ó hEithir's *Over the Bar* tied together the intimate details of personal experience with the sweep of history on a global scale, offering a way into both. Near the book's beginning, he wrote of being a boy in the Aran Islands on a September Sunday in 1939, the day World War II began after Hitler's invasion of Poland, and the day also of one the most famous All-Ireland hurling finals in history. It was a signal moment in his childhood: 'The All-Ireland hurling final of 1939 will always be remembered as the Thunder and Lightning Final. The elements gave a fitting welcome to that morning's declaration of war, and bangs and crashes punctuated Michael O'Hehir's commentary, as we sat with heads inclined towards the radio in my aunt Annie's kitchen in Inis Mór. It was doubly difficult to follow the game as the kitchen was full of old women who had come to hear news of the war and who moaned and prayed and sobbed at each peal and flash. I can still see the women and smell their sodden shawls. I couldn't comprehend their grief, for at the age of nine a world war seemed a more exciting prospect, even than an All-Ireland final.'

## A Gambler

On Christmas Eve 2019, two emails arrived from paddypower.com. The timing was awful – the emails were a profound source of irritation. In the greater scheme of things, they might be considered to be standard fare, primarily advertising the fact that there were gambles to be made on the Christmas horse race meetings and on soccer matches. There was also an invitation to join Paddy's Rewards Club, where a certain number of bets, worth a certain value, would entitle me to a free bet. Enough gambling would entitle me to enter a draw to win tickets to the Super Bowl.

There was, finally, a reminder that there was money sitting in my account – and that it might as well be used. I had opened an account with paddypower.com back sometime in 2002 or thereabouts. If I have made fifty bets since then I'd be amazed. The amounts gambled would almost never have been much more than €5 – months and even years passed between bets.

The balance on the account on Christmas Eve was about €240.05 – I reckon that is more or less the amount that was put in originally, combined with possibly two other deposits. As best I can remember, if I was down at all, it was no more than €40 or €50. I may well have been slightly up.

So, basically, gambling is a very small thing in my life. I've received hundreds of emails from Paddy Power and never been irritated by them; they were essentially irrelevant to me and went unopened into the email bin. Not this time, though. This time the arrival of two emails provoked a definite course of action: I decided straightaway to find a way to withdraw all the funds in my account and to shut it down. To be fair to paddypower.com, withdrawing the cash and shutting down the account was easily achieved and was assisted by helpful staff over the phone.

The cause of the irritation and of the desire to shut down my Paddy Power account was a really simple one – I had just read Declan Lynch and Tony O'Reilly's book *Tony 10: The Astonishing Story of the Postman who Gambled €10,000,000 … and Lost It All*. I cannot think of a more important book ever written on any aspect of Irish sport. It tells the story of Tony O'Reilly, a postman from Carlow who moved from being an occasional gambler to one who became grotesquely addicted. His gambling career stretched from the days of the old-style bookie's office to the modern internet-based account. Those early days in bookies' offices connected O'Reilly to a world that stretched back into the nineteenth century and beyond. It can be found, for example, in Charles Dickens' brilliant book, *Night Walks*.

This book, published in the Penguin Books 'Great Ideas' collection, pulled together miscellaneous writings from the time in the life of Dickens when he was struggling with insomnia and spent night after night walking the streets of London. He documented what he saw on those walks and these pages – together with other miscellaneous bits of journalism written between 1850 and 1870 – include a chilling short piece, entitled simply 'Betting Shops'. This piece sets out the inside of betting shops in Victorian Britain and the essentials of the story – rich men and poor men in thrall to gambling, sometimes winning but more usually losing, their lives given to the next wager – remain at the core of the story of betting. Indeed, the fundamental place of that wager in the very existence of so many men is easily observed.

It is true – then and now – that there are many who can flit in and out of that world as they wish, who can control the gamble and use it to add another dimension to their enjoyment of sport. Nobody can argue against that. But, equally, nobody can deny that the story told in *Tony 10* illustrates with devastating clarity – detail piled upon detail until full ruination looms in view, its inevitability rendering the story all the more compelling – the way gambling has changed. In its changing it has cultivated a phenomenon so insidious, so pervasive that its mental scourge is beyond cruel.

That you can now gamble on so many things from the phone in your pocket and that you can continue to ruin yourself at any hour of the day or night is a simple fact; it changes everything about gambling. You no longer have to walk into a betting shop to impale yourself on your addiction – you can do it anywhere and anytime, simply by reaching into your pocket and taking out your phone.

Writing this book must have been an incredibly painful experience for Tony O'Reilly. He seeks no vindication in the text and blames nobody else. The book does not preach, nor does it seek to court your sympathy. Instead, it centres on telling the story of a man who built for himself two worlds. In one of those worlds, he was Tony O'Reilly, husband, father, well-known man about Carlow, and post office manager. In the other, he was Tony 10, the name he used to gamble under when online. The story of the book is the story of how Tony 10 colonised the life of Tony O'Reilly, until he was left with mere fragments of what he once was and once had. In the process, he caused immense hurt to those whom he loved the most.

Reading his story has been a transformative experience. But where can this transformation go? How do you act on a truth revealed? The world has not begun to grapple in any meaningful way with the meaning of what it is to gamble in the age of the internet. Back in the nineteenth century, Charles Dickens believed that the answer was not to be found in legislative intervention. That is not now a sustainable position.

But impactful legislative action will require imagination and courage – is there a policymaker out there fit to take up the fight and win? Even with legislation there is a dire need for a broad information campaign on gambling – without this education, the stories of lives ruined by bets will only grow and grow. The centrality of gambling to sporting culture is obvious and undeniable. As sporting culture is ubiquitous in our modern life, this has a profound relevance to our society.

Back for a minute to those two emails that came from paddypower.com. They're entitled to send them, of course; they are in the business of making as much money as they can. Although for them to make money, I must lose. And you must lose. As much as possible. So what they did was legal and in keeping with their goals around profit. They can rightly point out, too, that you can close your account and you can unsubscribe.

Although, that is not how addiction ordinarily works. Even if it was, there is the fact of two emails in the space of an hour on Christmas Eve. You'd wonder how much damage receiving them could do to an addicted mind, on the day that's in it, with all that that could mean to the lives of those who live around that addict. Here, at least – viewed through the prism of Tony 10 – nothing ever brought home so clearly the reach of modern bookmakers into the minds and lives of their customers; and nothing demonstrated so brutally their relentless pursuit of profit.

## Killing Giraffes

It is not clear how the book given in the 1890s as a prize to C.I. Clarke made it to a shelf in the second-hand section of Chapters bookshop in Dublin. The book is James Greenwood's *Wild Sports of the World*. It is more than 120 years old and is rooted in those years when the British Empire was at the zenith of its power.

A badge pinned inside its front cover told the story of its origins; it recorded that on 5 April 1896, the president of the local Young Men's Christian Association (YMCA), Henry Whitwell, presented it as a prize at a meeting in Birmingham. The prize was given to one C. I. Clarke to mark his regularity of appearance at YMCA meetings over the previous half-year.

The stories of Clarke and Whitwell have disappeared from history – but the book that passed between them survives in mint condition. Its author, James Greenwood, was one of the great pioneering investigative journalists of the Victorian Age. For example, he dressed as a 'tramp' and was admitted to a London workhouse in the 1860s. The piece he wrote –

'A Night in the Workhouse' – was a raw, unsanitised account of what he encountered. It caused a sensation.

There is something of a dispute over whether – as a writer – Greenwood was genuinely concerned about the lives of the people he wrote about, or whether he was so driven by pursuit of fame that he exploited some and exaggerated about others. That is the kind of dispute that has swirled around the lives of many journalists ever since. Nonetheless, Greenwood was acknowledged as an important writer and his works were published and republished.

Greenwood's *Wild Sports of the World* was a different kind of book to his previous undercover work, however. Indeed, it is an extraordinary book. It could only have been written at the highpoint of British imperialism. It is soaked in the rhetoric of empire and is just about the last period of time in history in which somebody could write about 'sports' of the world as constituting only the hunt of big game.

To set up his book, Greenwood makes the claim that the 'secret of the vast successes' of the empire had its source in adventure: 'It is simply an historical fact that England was born of adventure.' He continued by writing of his hope that 'for the world's sake, as well as our own' this spirit of adventure will live for many more years. Naturally, the idea of 'colonisation' was a good thing for Greenwood, with its 'subjugation of territory and the supplanting of less useful races'. More than anything else, the book is a plea for 'manliness and pluck' – the sort of manliness and pluck that was supposed to underpin the whole notion of the British Empire of sport from soccer to rugby, and from cricket to polo.

In setting out a purpose of his book, Greenwood rests it on his hope that 'the excitement to be found in its pages cannot fail to stimulate the more wholesome, more generous, more manly instincts of those into whose hands it is destined to fall'.

It's not known if C.I. Clarke read the book with which he was presented and was moved to pursue a life of 'manliness'. Nor is it clear that he was moved by it to travel around the world to pursue the sports that are set out. But if he were so moved, he would have killed an awful lot of animals.

For example, the first chapters tell stories of how Englishmen have hunted to death great numbers of elephants, lions, pumas, gorillas, rhinos, tigers, hippos, leopards, panthers, jaguars, buffalos and kangaroos (to name but a few). The book has the illusion of being somewhat educational – there are guidelines on the physical constitution of each of the animals, and on their natural habitats, before discourse on the actual hunt is considered.

In this discourse, first-hand testimony of those who have undertaken the hunting is given an airing. Sometimes this testimony comes from English explorers, other times it comes from 'savage hunters'. Where would a book set at the high point of British imperialism be without reference to local 'savages'?

The descriptions of how people hunted are filled with detail. For example, down in Africa, live ostriches were hunted for feathers by locals who disguised themselves in the skin of a dead ostrich and stalked about the plain imitating their walk. In other parts, they were hunted by Arabs on horseback or were caught in traps. For their part, the method most favoured by imperialists was to wait by watering holes for the ostriches to appear. As they drank the water, slowly and deliberately, taking great big gulps, they were shot with high-powered rifles.

There is also the story of Major Gordon and the mighty giraffe family he encountered while out hunting game: 'Having brought down one of them with a musket-ball, the Major approached, and stroked the animal's forehead, and otherwise caressed it, when so far from exhibiting resentment or anger, the poor brute gently closed its eyes as though grateful for the caress.'

But even someone as lacking in self-awareness as Major Gordon could not deny the downside to this particular death: 'When its throat was cut, preparatory to taking off the skin, the giraffe, while struggling in the last agonies, struck the ground convulsively with its feet with immense force, as it looked reproachfully on its assailant with its eyes fast glazing with the film of death.'

Not that this brought any pause for reflection in the book.

In the next sentence, we are off with Sir William Harris to kill more giraffes, this time in central Africa. Seeing some thirty-two giraffes feasting on leaves in a flowering mimosa grove, Sir William 'knew they were mine'. Sitting on his horse, he loaded and fired, and loaded and fired, continuing to shoot even as his target shuffled and stumbled into death.

The dying giraffe was 'mute, dignified and majestic', it had 'tears trickling from the lashes of his dark humid eyes', while as Sir William described 'broadside after broadside was poured into his brawny front'. And then came death.

For Sir William it was the finest trophy he ever won and the dying breath of the giraffe brought absolute joy: 'Never shall I forget the intoxicating excitement of that moment!'

The great myth of the British Empire was the supposed nobility of its civilising mission. This mission was soaked in the images of Christianity and in the so-called manliness of its sports. As justifications go, it was utterly warped and self-serving and plainly false. Sometimes it takes the image of a dying giraffe, its life taken by a hail of bullets fired from a bloodthirsty English colonial, to remember the hubris of those who celebrate the culture of an empire that took from the world as it wished.

## Roy of the Rovers

It cannot be easy to play at the top level of English soccer for more than six decades.

But the great Roy Race is still going strong.

Roy made his debut for Melchester Rovers back in 1954. He was then just another young footballer trying to make his way in the game and his first steps were traced in the pages of the *Tiger* comic. That comic – 'a sport and adventure picture story weekly' – was launched on 11 September 1954.

Boys' adventure comics were a hugely popular type of comic in Britain during the 1950s and 1960s. Their combined sales reached beyond 500 million a year and they became the staple reading fare of a generation of young readers, colonising the imagination. The comics came in a variety of forms and many focused heavily on stories of British heroism, not least during World War II. The simplistic comic-book legend of that heroism is still a defining aspect of modern British life.

'Roy of the Rovers' featured in that first edition of *Tiger* in 1954 – and he went on to become the finest player in English soccer history. The comic traced his emergence from schoolboy soccer in the 1950s, before he truly flourished in the 1960s when he matured into a rugged, square-jawed hero, a shock of blond hair sitting gloriously on his head. Of course, his image changed over the years: his hair got longer and then shorter and then longer; sideburns came and went; and his shorts went high up the thigh and then back down again.

It was only in 1976 that 'Roy of the Rovers' graduated from the pages of *Tiger*. Then, for more than 800 issues, Roy Race grew to become an iconic figure in modern English culture, with his own comic. This transcended sport. Someone who had achieved the impossible – achieved a thing that was almost undreamed of – was considered to have engaged in 'real Roy of the Rovers stuff'.

At its peak, the comic sold one million copies a week in Britain and Ireland. Its arrival into shops on Saturday mornings was a vital moment in the early lives of many children.

Naturally, Roy Race stood for something more than just being a star player. He believed in 'playing the right way'. That is to say, his soccer was a triumph of style and of fair play. In the context of English soccer in the 1970s and 1980s, this was no mean achievement. Rarely has a man so successful been so entirely out of keeping with the mores of his age.

As he grew from boy to man, Roy married his childhood sweetheart Penny Laine and they had three kids. All the while he was starring for Melchester Rovers as they rose through the ranks of English soccer, winning leagues and cups. Indeed, Roy Race won some nine league titles, eight FA Cups, three League Cups, three European Cups, one UEFA Cup, and four Cup Winners' Cups. At the heart of these successes was his capacity to score the last-minute winner.

Naturally, all of this success earned Roy the call to play for the national team. Eventually, in 1978 he was prevailed upon to become player-manager of England. The team he selected depended heavily on his teammates at Melchester Rovers, but also included stars of the English game such as Trevor Francis.

But it was not all glory. Part of Roy Race's greatness was his capacity to overcome adversity. In an edition entitled 'The Great Melchester Massacre', the Rovers' bus was attacked by terrorists in the (previously unknown) Middle Eastern country of Basran. Most of the squad was killed and Roy was a lucky man to escape. There's no room here to set out the sheer scale of things that went wrong for Roy in his career. There were repeated kidnappings. The summer tours to South America proved particularly risky – no sooner would the players be off the plane than kidnappers would be binding their hands with ropes and writing ransom notes. But, even worse than the kidnappings were the shootings – most particularly the outrageous attempt on Roy's life in December 1981 when he was shot and almost died. 'Who shot Roy Race?' became one of the great questions of the age. It was a year after J.R. Ewing had been shot in *Dallas*.

There was also the trauma of the earthquake that followed from a collapsed mine which destroyed Mel Park. Melchester Rovers were forced to play their games at Wembley Stadium. There was enormous exuberance (and relief) when they were able to return to a rebuilt Mel Park in February 1989.

The 1990s were tough for Roy. It is true that English soccer was remade in that decade with the creation of the Premier League but Roy of the Rovers struggled to keep pace. His son, Rocky, made it into the team, but the reality was that comic books could not now compete with video games and other more high-tech pastimes which became central to modern popular culture. The *FIFA International Soccer* video game, first released in 1993, offered too much competition. A *Roy of the Rovers* computer game was released for play on early computers but it didn't really take off.

Attempts to keep pace with more modern storylines did not bring any joy. In the mid-1990s, the comic moved from weekly to monthly. Then it was pulled altogether, before making a comeback in 1997 as part of the *Match of the Day* magazine. In the end, and in the aftermath of a shocking helicopter crash which left him needing to have his left foot amputated, the career of Roy of the Rovers was ended in 2001.

There seemed no way back.

But where Roy of the Rovers is concerned, the mere amputation of a foot could never prove too much of a challenge. So it is that Roy is back now – and he's young again. Roy's new life in the graphic novels is the product of the efforts of a new publisher, Rebellion. Roy Race is a part-time carer for his disabled father trying to make his way into the game with Melchester Rovers. The club is mired in the lower leagues – the perfect environment for a teenage prodigy to launch a glorious career. The new novels also show the young striker trying to cope with the demands of social media, of agents and of the challenges of modern celebrity. Entitled *Kick-Off* and *Foul Play*, they also have Roy back doing what he does best – scoring goals.

Accompanying the novels is a collection by Andy Jacobs entitled simply *Roy of the Rovers*. This book charts the making of a modern footballing institution as a sort of Roy of the Rovers 65th Anniversary Special. There are goals and glory and it is all bathed in the warm glow of nostalgia for a time and for a type of person that only ever existed in the pages of comic books. Most of all, the comics are just harmless fun and reading them is a fine way to pass time.

# 14 MEMORIES

eclan Murphy was riding Arcot at Haydock Park on Monday, 2 May 1994 in the 2pm race, the Crowther Homes Swinton Handicap Hurdle. Arcot was the favourite and as he approached the last fence of the race, he was up to third place, having made his way through the pack. To win, he needed an exceptional jump at the last. What unfolded instead was a disaster. The horse crashed into the hurdle, the skulls of horse and jockey collided, and Murphy was unconscious even before he hit the ground. He was then galloped over by the horses following behind, and the hoof of Cockney Lad hit him flush in the head. Murphy broke his skull in twelve places, had the last rites read to him and his obituary was made ready for printing in the *Racing Post*. But he did not die and eventually he woke from the coma into which he had fallen. But when he came back, he was – by his own testimony – a changed man. Among the changes were that the memories of more than four years of his life between October 1989 and May 1994 had essentially been destroyed.

Some two decades later he agreed to tell his story. But how do you put back that memory when writing a book? How do you recount races that you do not remember riding in? Murphy worked with Ami Rao to produce *Centaur* ('the memoir of a jockey who came back from the dead') through painstaking research of archives, news clippings, viewings of YouTube videos, and conversations with people. Races were considered over and over again, from multiple perspectives. Murphy and Rao wrote: 'We reconstruct them like two Picassos, frame by frame, fence by fence. We objectify, analyse and fracture. We disrupt the notion of traditional autobiography, we mock the "I", we take apart the neatly packaged illusion of perspective. And then, once we have adequately destroyed, we proceed to rebuild. We begin to create *Centaur*. We connect dots, draw lines and take leaps. We reconstruct and reassemble, fusing together past and present, my life, my truth, her perspective, her biases, slowly stitching together the patches of pride that made up those years of glory.' So it is that *Centaur* emerged as 'an intricate reconstructed collage where real things are embedded within, and enhanced by, the fiction of the mind'. The abandonment of a 'generic recounting of how a sportsman remembers his career' was rendered inevitable by the accident and the memory loss that Murphy suffered. But how do you describe the book – is it real or invented? And how has the process of making the book impacted on Murphy's mind? 'Little bits come back to me as I relive the races, but whether it is memory or imagination, I will never know.'

## Pool Tables

Marielle Viera has left her desk and is looking for the parcel of books that has arrived by courier. It's stacked somewhere on one of the desks that are exactly where the pool tables used to sit in the middle of the Belfield Bar. I slip into a daydream while I'm waiting. It's 1991 and myself and Johnny Keville are playing pool on one of those tables. It's Winners Stay On and we've been here for hours now, holding the table against all comers and drinking pints of Bass. The Bass is 92p a pint on special offer. And we are now feeling very special ourselves. I've long hair and I'm wearing dungarees. I'm also wearing a pair of red bootrunners that Johnny has defaced with slurs suggesting that I may be a little bit pretentious. He's not wrong! But I'm only twenty and anyway I can't wash the ink off. We hold the pool table all evening. At least in the dream we do.

But the Belfield Bar isn't a bar anymore. It has been renamed Building 71. The bottom half of the building is now set out for exams. There's even a whiteboard erected up where the long bar counter once supported elbow after elbow. The top end of the bar, where the bands used to play, is now used for storing dozens of huge cardboard boxes. And it's used also for taking in courier packages on a near-deserted campus in the time of Covid.

Marielle is looking still for my books. So I dream on, deeper this time. It's 1988 and I walk into that bar for the first time. I get an unreal surge of wonder. The word to describe the atmosphere in the bar that day has yet to be invented. There are men – well, boys, who will be men – hanging upside down on the steel beams that run below the ceiling using the curve of their knees. Other boys, and girls who will be women, are passing them up pints and they're drinking them upside down. I don't remember reading about it in the college prospectus. They are ag students or maybe engineers and they're all from the country, loose in the city; their world has been remade. I'm with Éanna O'Sullivan from Taobh a' Chnoic, Brandon in Co. Kerry. We've come over from an Irish class. It's the middle of the afternoon. I'm about to grow up an awful lot in the time it takes to drink two pints. At least I think it was just two pints. Three at most. Maybe four. We were in no position to play pool, but we put our money down on the table. Our turn came. It was short and brutal. By the third humiliation, we'd had enough. There's a tipping point where playing pool is not feasible.

Marielle is back with my books. You've to sign for them, she says. We're both wearing masks. She has an easy laugh and it takes any formality out of things. I tell her that it used to be a bar here and she has the manners to pretend it is the first time she has heard this. I walk down towards the old dancefloor before leaving, just for a look, to see if the old grime and grunge linger still. The shutters on the bar counter are partly open. I wonder are Seamus or Dec in there, and do they still have Bass. And in my head, all I can hear is Primal Scream. Bobby Gillespie is singing 'Damaged':

'The way I felt inside
Made me feel so glad to be alive
Got damaged
I got damaged,'

sings Bobby. Sweat and a boundless raw energy hang in the air. I know that this night won't end here. There is a party in a flat in Ranelagh. And I don't have to get up in the morning, if there is a morning. Or maybe not even in the afternoon. Because time now has no limit.

I say thank you to Marielle, leave the bar – or Building 71 – and I head back across the campus to my office. UCD is a different place; the wildness is gone. But as I walk, the ghosts of that wildness are everywhere; the years run one into the next. I head down past Theatre L in the Newman Building and remember how nervous I was the first time I sat in a lecture in there. Barely seventeen, knowing nobody, magnificently clueless, just starting out.

I remember also how nervous I was the first time I taught in there. Five hundred and twenty seats full of history students. And me in front of them, about to find out a lot about becoming something different in front of a crowd.

I walk on past the Blob, as the ambiguous sculpture in the middle of the arts concourse is still called. I wonder does anyone arrange to meet there, like we used to – at the Blob – now that everyone has a smartphone. I know the answer before that question is even fully formed.

Down the stairs from the Blob is the great windowless cave of joy that was the Trap. This was a room that held a dozen pool tables and was ringed by video game machines. Now blocked off and fenced off by in lurid yellow, it holds the unmarked graves of many degrees.

I go up into my office and pull asunder the parcel of books that Marielle has given me. I open the *Dictionary of Imaginary Places*. It's a magical book. There are brilliant entries on Dracula's castle and Freedonia from the Marx Brothers' film *Duck Soup* and on hundreds of other pretend lands of film and literature and folklore. The Belfield Bar hasn't made this edition of the dictionary, but it, too, is now an imaginary place, created and recreated only in the memory of generations of students, an imagined land where nobody can get old.

## The Boiler

The ball is about to turn under the crossbar down at the Railway End goals. The raindrops will soon be shaking from the net. Charlie Nelligan will be on the ground in a heap and the umpire will reach for the green flag.

Seamus Darby will launch into a joyous jig and the man in the yellow oilskin jacket in the old sideline seats in front of the Hogan Stand will join him. The man in the yellow oilskin jacket is my father. Beside him is my younger brother David. The two of them are already standing as the ball enters the goal.

All around them, others are climbing out of their seats. This is the goal that will win the 1982 All-Ireland football final for Offaly: the most famous one-in-a-row in GAA history.

Colman Doyle caught the moment in a photograph taken from in front of Hill 16. I've brought that photograph to every place I've lived in.

It is that most rare of things: a moment caught in time when you see your dreams about to be made real. That my father is in the photograph makes it all the better.

A few minutes after Seamus Darby's goal, the final whistle has blown and Offaly fans have breached the wire in front of the Hogan Stand.

There's men and women and children of all shapes and sizes getting under the wire and over it and through it. They're piling in from the Cusack Stand side too, and from Hill 16 and the Canal End.

There's a glorious madness to the crowd as the RTÉ cameras pan across the pitch.

It's pouring rain and the man in the yellow oilskins is spinning round in a manic state: who knows what he's trying to do, but it's great fun watching him do it.

It's also great fun looking at that footage for my brother and not seeing him: my father has lost him (or better still forgotten him) in the clamour. No harm: that should have been me in the sideline seat beside my father!

I'd been sitting on my own up in the back corner of the stand, delighted to have the freedom to be with myself, but disgusted that a younger brother had bested me.

Now, though, the game is over and I'm out on the pitch. I see my mother and I head towards her. Before I get there, Seamus Darby picks her up and throws her in the air. And then he does it again. He's from Rhode and she's from Rhode, and no further explanation is needed.

Seamus Darby has just scored the greatest goal of all time to win the greatest match of all time on the greatest day of all time.

And there it ends. I don't remember the presentation of the cup or the speeches or leaving the pitch. All I remember is my mother driving myself and my brothers out to Finglas on the northside of Dublin.

My grandfather, Dick Conroy, lived there. Dick Conroy was known in his home village of Rhode and in certain parts of London as 'The Boiler'. He was a huge man, great fun and recklessly devoted to the GAA, especially to Offaly football.

He had played on the first minor team fielded by Offaly in 1928. Later he played for the senior team and had been a selector on the Offaly team defeated by Kerry in the 1969 All-Ireland final. He was my hero and I was definitely his favourite; he spoiled me magnificently.

When we arrived to the house, he was overcome by emotion, great tears streamed down his face, one after the next. He hugged my mother and hugged all of us.

I was twelve and I couldn't understand why he was crying; I understand now and I think of him whenever I see people crying after winning a match. It's about the match and it's about much more than the match.

He died two summers later, in 1984, of a broken heart. My nana had died eight weeks previously and he just didn't have any interest in living without her.

He was brought home to Rhode to be buried. Generations of footballers came up to pay their respects in a long, snaking line. In that line were men he had played football with and brought to football matches and given jobs on building sites – and men from the Offaly 1982 team. These everyday gods stood in place like all the others.

When the coffin left the backdoor of the church to be brought to the graveyard, a small group of men – among them Dermot O'Brien, a Tullamore man who remained one of the great stalwarts of London GAA – draped it with the flag of Round Towers, the club my granddad had been so involved in when he built houses in London in the 1950s and 1960s.

Dermot had come over from London for the funeral in the middle of the week when it wasn't cheap or easy to do so; the more I remember that act, the more wonderful I think it is. The Round Towers flag now lay beside the Offaly and the Rhode jerseys on that last journey.

That day, after the funeral, the pubs of Rhode overflowed with drink. All the while, myself and my brothers and my cousins and other boys from Rhode played football on a lawn in the village beside the Murphys' house.

Many years later, when myself and my brothers played championship football for Tullamore against those same cousins and their friends, no victory tasted more sweetly and no defeat hurt quite as badly. Maybe nobody else cared too much about our connection to Rhode, but it really mattered to us.

The evening after the funeral was a different type of football, though. The heat of the day had faded to the warmth of the night and the village was framed by a soft darkness. We played on for hour after hour, the sounds of the pubs hanging in the air around us. Nobody seemed in a rush to go anywhere.

And for us, as the leather flew back and across, we weren't dreaming of the future or thinking about The Boiler; we were just playing football.

# 15 COVID-19

The impact of the Covid-19 pandemic on sport was straightforward: organised sport essentially stopped as a collective realtime experience. The evidence for that was everywhere, from the leagues and championship abandoned across multiples sports, to the closed grounds and the television channels left only with nostalgia reels of old events. But it is a paradoxical truth that sporting and leisure activities appear to have never been higher than at a time when sporting organisation could not run their activities. This was made clear from a survey produced several months into the first lockdown in Ireland. That survey documented a huge increase in walking, running, cycling and so on. This was clearly a product of quieter roads, working from home, having more time and other related aspects of the lockdown. That's very interesting to consider, and should be of particular interest to funding agencies who give money to sporting bodies to promote matters of public health. It may also have interesting long-term implications for, say, private gyms or swimming pools; it begs the question as to why precisely a person would go to a gym or a pool when you can use free weights out in the open or if you live close enough to swim in the sea.

Obviously, the most profound impact of Covid-19 was the lives that were lost and the manner in which it left people with long-term health problems to manage. But a further significant impact was the manner in which people questioned the nature of their lives. This was clearly something that was dependent on the nature of a person's pre-Covid life, of their disposable income, and of their home circumstances. It is something different than the colour pieces which appeared in the newspapers and on websites talking about fundamental changes in human behaviour and of people 'never again going back' to the old way of living. It was rooted in a sense that life had become too busy, too filled with working and commuting, and with organised social interactions of numerous different types, including sport.

The questions people asked of their lives are, of course, specific to their own world. For some, it ended in a determination never to return to work fulltime in an office, but to spend at least some time working from home. For others, as the 'novelty' of having to stay at home wore off, the answer was manifest in a desire that the life they had previously enjoyed should be recreated as soon as possible, or at least as fully as possible. Because, even if they hadn't truly enjoyed their pre-Covid existence, the reality of life in Covid was much worse, not just financially but also socially. The scale of the disruption to life, the manner in which patterns of living were so fundamentally disrupted, forced reappraisals even if none were necessarily sought. Once the questions start, they ordinarily keep coming.

## Home

What does home mean?

When you're from the country but you live and work in Dublin, it usually means two places. The house in whatever part of Dublin you live in, and also the place where you grew up. That word 'home' is applied to both, it just means different things.

No matter how long I live in Dublin, I still talk of 'going home'. That home is a house on a side of the esker that runs east-west across Ireland. I think about that house every day; it sits in the area called Durrow, in the parish of Tullamore, in Co. Offaly. It's where my parents live. It's where myself and my three brothers were formed. It's a place which runs through me no matter where I am or what I do.

Then in Covid, there was no going home. That was a strange thing, dislocating and unpleasant. There were times before when I was unable to just go home when I wanted, times when I lived in England and in Italy. But that was the consequence of decisions I had made for myself. In Covid, not being allowed go home by public health rules was different. But it was not just about rules. I could not go home because I did not want to infect my parents with something that could kill them.

Covid made me think too often and for too long of the road west out of Dublin. There, along that stretch of the M6, with Kinnegad behind me through the mirrors, stands my favourite sculpture in the world: moons and half-moons erect on tall poles. I love those moons, and I love them because of what I see between them and behind them. The land stretches back, long and flat and brown, onto Croghan Hill, which itself stands majestic above the bog. We learned in school that Croghan Hill was an extinct volcano – a great and exotic fact that has stuck when so much else has disappeared into an oblivion of lost schooling. We were also told it was a magnificent place from which to look down on our neighbours in Westmeath and Kildare, those who were by place of birth self-evidently less fortunate than us. As kids, we were proud of the glamour of having an extinct volcano in our county, and I was also proud of the bog. There it is still, stretching out behind the moons and half-moons, full of secrets and deception. Of course, my Offaly 'home' is an imaginary place. It's not just the place where my parents and one brother still live, or the physical existence of the house where I grew up. It's also the prism of memory.

Even as things opened up in the mid-summer of 2020, there was a strain to life that was restrictive. This was eased a small bit when the Offaly senior football championship started. The coverage of the games on Offaly Faithful TV meant a connection that went beyond sport. When Tullamore made it – against the odds – to play defending champions Ferbane in the county semi-final, it proved the sporting highlight of a putrid year. The Tullamore team, led by the brilliant John Moloney and managed by my friends, included veterans with whom I had played senior football fifteen years ago and new bloods, boys who were the sons of other men I'd played with. The sense of having ties to this new team was real, not imagined – it was something rooted in old friendships and a shared history on that same field.

But there was also another layer to this day: All the way through the match, right up to the final whistle, and beyond it into two periods of extra time, the roaring that came out through the speakers on the computer was unreal. In co-commentary, the then Offaly senior football manager, John Maughan, observed with an admiring laugh how loud and emotional the Tullamore crowd were as they rode the madness of a contest that swung one way and then the next. The few Tullamore supporters who had managed to get into the ground under Covid-19 restrictions were really on it, behind their team and the way they were playing, from the minute the ball was thrown in. It got louder and louder as the game went on. I knew those voices. I could pick them out. One of them was a brother. Others were men I had played football with for Tullamore. Others again were voices that had roared at me when I was playing. It was an extraordinary experience. Watching that game on a computer screen was an exquisite pain. To have that union with place and people was a wonderful thing; to not be there was a small cruelty.

In the raw drama of the inevitable penalty shoot-out, the computer came alive. Everything else was irrelevant. All that mattered was the ball and the net.

After twenty penalty kicks, we won. Many lifetimes were lived in that sentence.

The outpouring of joy in O'Connor Park, the sight of men in blue jumping with a wildness that no passage of the years can control, was replicated at the far end of an ethernet cable, in a Dublin kitchen, where two homes collided.

## Fr Tom

The fire is burning hot in the hearth and there is a card game is full swing.

There is noise. Endless noise. Happy noise.

My granddad and nana are playing, so it has to be before 1983. My father and mother are playing. Bridie Murphy is playing. Our next-door neighbour, Tom Ravenhill, a serious card-player, is playing. Fr Tom Scully is playing.

I, too, am sitting at the big table for the first time, the eight hand, up out of the bed to be dealt a hand of cards. I'm sitting with my back to the fire, an eleven-year old man (or maybe ten), and the cards falling on the table. My three little brothers are all in bed, the only place for them.

It's late into the evening. The game, of course, is twenty-five and it's serious. But it's only serious because it's a chance to poke. And poke. And keep on poking until there's a reaction.

Fr Tom is home from England and he's at the centre of it all. Many people walk through our front door, but there is nobody like Fr Tom.

He is a mathematician, sharp and precise and clear. But that's not it, or at least not all of it. He has a charisma and an energy and a way of being positive that fills a room in a way that is utterly unique.

His only interest in the card-game tonight is winding up my granddad – Dick 'The Boiler' Conroy. They have a long and wonderful friendship that is rooted in football, and Fr Tom knows exactly how to get The Boiler to blow.

He goads my granddad about how he didn't rate such-and-such a footballer – and a year later that man was an All-Star. And is now acclaimed as one of the greats.

The bait swings through the air. The Boiler knows he's being goaded. He knows he needs to ignore it. But he can't. The steam is too much. The lid comes off. The room convulses again.

\* \* \*

It's 1969 and Fr Tom Scully walks into the Offaly senior football dressing-room. Through the 1960s he has trained Belcamp College in Dublin. In these years, that boarding school for boys, also a juniorate for the Oblate Fathers, has won three Leinster schools football championships – taking down the old powers such as St Mel's of Longford.

He has also trained many Offaly players living in the city, driving them in famously tough sessions.

Now he is back down in Tullamore, the man newly in charge of an intercounty team that is stuck in a rut. There are veteran players who were bitterly unlucky to lose to Down in the 1961 All-Ireland final – men like Paddy McCormack and Greg Hughes and the team captain Johnny Egan.

There are also younger men such as Martin Furlong and Tony McTeague and Willie Bryan who had won the county its only All-Ireland minor football title in 1964.

But they are stuck. The optimism of the early 1960s has given way to a sort of torpor that hangs over the team.

When Fr Tom goes to the clubroom at O'Connor Park in Tullamore to meet the players for the first time, he is struck by how miserable the mood is. There are players who are talking about retirement and other players who are about to emigrate.

A county board official tells him that he is wasting his time.

But Fr Tom never wastes time. He sets about getting the players to train hard. And train they do.

He just has a way with people and they want to play better for him. He's really astute on the field. He shifts the team around, tries new approaches, just as he had with Belcamp, and they prosper in the spring.

From nowhere, Offaly make a National Football League final for the first time in its history. They are hammered by Kerry, 3–11 to 0–8, and that's disappointing, but it's no disaster. The upswing is there for all to see.

The spirit in the team is growing; his bond with the players is tightening. He gives a few of the players, led by Willie Bryan, the loan of his car to go to Athlone. They drink pints and pints. They bring the car back to his house intact – and Fr Tom drops them back into town for more pints.

He lends the car more than once that summer.

The months roll on and Offaly cruise through the Leinster championship – no team gets within five points of them. It is only the third time ever that Offaly have won the Leinster championship.

Cavan take them to a replay in the All-Ireland semi-final, but that replay is won and it's back to a rematch with Kerry.

Offaly are much better now in September than they were back in the spring. Fr Tom thinks they will beat Kerry. More than that, he believes they will. Fully believes.

But on the day, it doesn't happen. Offaly play poorly and lose a disappointing final by 0–10 to 0–7.

It is Fr Tom's last real match as Offaly manager; by early

1970 he is sent to teach maths in Johannesburg. He hates the system, hates apartheid, gets out as quickly as he can.

\* \* \*

It's May 1988. The RTÉ cameras are in Camden Town and Fr Tom is talking to the reporter, Leo Enright. Fr Tom is now the Director of the Irish Centre in London, and a new wave of Irish emigrants has filled London's streets.

Fr Tom is running services to help those people adjust to a new life, drawing them into to a network where those who need it can be supported.

But he also has another plan. He has been in London for nearly two decades now and he has seen the way life has pulled at that wave of emigrants who had come to the city in the 1940s and 1950s.

He doesn't just lament it, he confronts it.

So he sets up a day centre in the Irish Centre to cater for more than 150 older people, giving lunch and a place to chat and play cards and take classes.

Most of the people in the centre are Irish, but some are English or from across Europe. He wants them to mix together to understand each other, to understand the different cultures.

Many times, Fr Tom says that loneliness is a thing that knows no nationality. This day centre is a way to beat down the loneliness.

\* \* \*

They didn't believe, he says. They didn't believe. Actually, no. Most of them believed. But a couple didn't, and that's why we lost.

It's 2018. Fr Tom is back in the front-room where the cards were played nearly four decades previously. His sight is as good as gone. Bridie Murphy has brought him over.

He's talking about why Offaly lost to Kerry in 1969. The cut of that defeat is still felt. He's not consumed by it – nothing as ridiculous as that. His life has carried too much to be defined or soured by a lost match.

But his whole body rises with his words, as he explains again why Offaly lost. Most of all, he still can't understand that any of his players could not believe. He's up in the chair, alive, back running through the game, as if it can be changed, as if time's arrow can be reversed.

There are no cards played, but the mind is as lucid as ever. He tells stories about London and Belcamp, about The Boiler and Nan. He laughs at the memory of The Boiler, a selector with him on the sideline in 1969, tormented beside the dugout in front of the Cusack Stand, arguing and arguing for a change to be made.

That great, wild laugh fills the room.

But he doesn't just talk and tell stories, he also listens. And he asks.

What is wrong with Offaly football. Why is it where it is? Why did you not beat Clare in the All-Ireland qualifiers?

Did they not believe, he asks? Did you not believe?

\* \* \*

It's a Tuesday morning in April 2020 and Darren Frehill is on *Morning Ireland* on RTÉ radio. Fr Tom Scully, who trained Offaly to reach the All-Ireland football final in 1969, has died, he says.

Pat Nolan writes a fine tribute in the *Irish Mirror*. In that tribute, one of Fr Tom's players, Eugene Mulligan, laments the loss of his old trainer: 'He was down at Mick O'Rourke's funeral, he was down at Johnny Egan's funeral, all the things that had happened, Fr Scully would be knocking around. He was definitely a players' man and the sad thing about it is, he's going to his grave and not one of us can be near it to pay him some bit of respect, which saddens me anyway and I know it saddens a lot of other fellas as well. We'd stand on our heads for him.'

The county chairman, Michael Duignan, says on Twitter that he was a 'brilliant man who helped so many people during his life, particularly Irish people who fell on hard times in London. A great ambassador for Offaly throughout his life and a very proud GAA man who was also a mighty chat and very easy company.'

All of that is true.

Fr Tom was less than a week in hospital, pulled down by the Covid-19 virus a month short of his ninetieth birthday. He was on the phone in the days before he went, endlessly positive, accepting of who he was and where he was. Believing to the end.

# 16 WAR IN UKRAINE

Nobody wrote like George Orwell. He was right about so much. But, of course, not about everything. When it came to writing about the relationship between sport and war, he had astute observations to make, but his basic thesis was wrong. In his essay 'The Sporting Spirit', Orwell wrote: 'At the international level sport is frankly mimic warfare.' This is an untypical lapse into popular nonsense that sporting contests are an imitation of war. This popular narrative is made plain in the language that is routinely used to describe matches: the language of battle, of defence and attack, of aerial bombardments, of fighting in the trenches, of howitzer boots and sniping and shots fired. And you can see why that language works as a lure to believing that war has been remade as sport. But the chasm between that belief and reality is vast.

The best thing that can be said is that at least Orwell didn't lapse into that other gross historical cliché that sport was promoted because it was essentially complementary to war, that it cultivated and sharpened warlike tendencies and, by extension, served an educative function in preparing people to fight. This notion is rooted in centuries of rhetoric that find their greatest exposition in phrases such as Duke of Wellington's supposed claim that the Battle of Waterloo was really won on the playing fields of Eton. Again, it is the kind of pithy claim that is appealing because it offers a neat explanation for both success in war and for the value of sport. But, of course, it is so flimsy as a theory that it collapses under the slightest scrutiny.

The context for Orwell's writing on sport and war offers some explanation for his frame of understanding. He wrote it in late 1945 in London in the aftermath of a war so brutal and so immersive that it almost defied comprehension. It was then exceptionally hard to look at any aspect of life and avoid seeing it through the blooded prism of the previous six years.

When Orwell was writing, a tour of Britain had just been undertaken by Dynamo Moscow. The tour ended with Dynamo beating Arsenal 4–3 in a match played in a thick fog before more than 50,000 people. There is footage of the match on YouTube – if you like looking at fog, it's a great watch. But still the crowd came and stayed, fuelled by an immense passion to go again to matches. The English leagues had stopped at the beginning of World War II and did not properly recommence until 1946. Orwell noted that at least two of the four matches played by Dynamo had ended in bad feeling and wrote: 'sport is an unfailing cause of ill-will, and ... if such a visit as this had any effect at all on Anglo-Soviet relations, it could only be to make them slightly worse than before.'

Of course, Orwell understood that sport was not the cause of the problem: 'I do not ... suggest that sport is one of the main causes of international rivalry; big-scale sport is itself, I think, merely another effect of the causes that have produced nationalism.' But he stuck to his point that sport did indeed 'make things worse'. To this end, he rightly laughed at what he called the 'blah-blahing about the clean, healthy rivalry of the football field and the great part played by the Olympic Games in bringing the nations together'.

Indeed, the notion that playing sport in some way replicates war or prepares you for war is trite and absurd. These are claims made, for example, by Admiral Lord Jellicoe, one of the Britain's military leaders from World War I. He believed that rugby was vital to the making of 'good fighting men'.

A great way of examining the merit of this claim is to look at those men – including international players – who went over the top of actual trenches rather than rolled around on a muddy field wrestling for possession. They died, one after the next, in a hail of bullets. Their bodies lie under white crosses on European fields or are mixed into the mud, with only their names surviving on the Thiepval Memorial. That memorial lists 72,000 names of men who lost their lives at the Battle of the Somme and have no known grave. They include men such as the Scottish rugby international Eric Milroy, who was one of more than thirty Scottish internationals to die in the war. His body was never found. He was twenty-nine when he died. In the slaughter of war, it is irrelevant if you have played rugby or the piano or poker or the fool or even the hero.

## Vladimir Putin and Sport

Everyone who loves sport has a personal story that explains this love. This is a story which is usually built into the sheer physical pleasure that comes from the act of playing.

The connection goes far beyond the physical. It is, instead, embedded in the meaning of their lives. Usually, also, there is a belief that sport is important to a person's values, that it has helped create a work ethic or sense of teamwork or volunteerism that has fed out into the rest of life, far beyond the boundaries of play. This is something that routinely appears in the life stories of people who find power or wealth in all walks of life. Sport is presented time and time again as a force for good, as an environment that facilitates noble behaviour and gives people the skills to walk from darkness towards light.

One of the people who has profited from this frame of representation is Vladimir Putin. Two decades ago, when he was consolidating his power in Russia, Putin spoke about his love of judo, how it gave him a philosophy that he could bring out into his life: 'I started practicing this sport when I was fourteen, and as a matter of fact, what I did start engaging in was something called sambo, which is a Russian acronym for "self-defence without arms", which is a Russian wrestling style. And, after that, I joined a gym that was teaching judo. And I was what they call a master of sports. We have our sporting ranks, and the equivalent of the black belt I received when I was, I guess, eighteen, in judo. And all my adult life I have been practicing judo and I do love the sport tremendously.'

Around this professed love of sport, Putin wrapped its

meaning to him, how it saved him from falling in darkness, and also how it taught him respect and a way of living: 'I think that there is more to it than just sport. I think it's also a philosophy in a way, and I think it's a philosophy that teaches one to treat one's partner with respect.'

Naturally enough, Putin continued to spout this nonsense year after year. He went further than that. He also 'co-authored' books about judo and took the lead role in a 2008 instructional video, aptly titled *Let's Learn Judo with Vladimir Putin.*

All the while, Putin has put himself at the centre of the story. There is footage of him scoring goals in an ice hockey match against global stars of the game, Putin in the frame with sporting celebrities at multiple events or, most revealingly of all, Putin bare-chested out hunting; the photographs are usually the staged attempts of a little man trying to pretend he's a bigger one.

Because many of us can identify with a love of sport and because we can understand what it has given to our own sense of self, we are susceptible to this manipulation. There is a universality to the idea of sport that transcends borders and language. In the year that this judo video was released, Putin had earlier led the Russian invasion of Georgia, with its catalogue of death, injury and the displacement of tens of thousands of innocent people.

The point here is that this notion that sport is an inherent force for good is complete sewage. It can help provide people with values – but not necessarily so. To presume that it does is a dangerous, misleading mistake.

For all of those warm and fuzzy stories of how sport has

provided people with a platform to behave with decency, there are many others which show the opposite. In sports clubs – and in their governing bodies, nationally and internationally – there are many brilliant people. But there have also been murderers, rapists, child abusers and villains of all stripes.

What is also interesting is the sense that sport is also supposed to help cultivate an understanding of people, a sort of practical humanity, to sit alongside the values that it is supposed to imbue. Too often, this too turns out to be rubbish. For example, in respect of Putin's latest war, decades of involvement in sport did not save Mick Wallace, MEP, from an abject failure of judgement. His position on Russia is such that it is hard to know where to start. Even after the scale of the Russian onslaught on Ukraine became plain, Wallace – once a TD and then an MEP – voted against a European Parliament resolution which condemned the Russian invasion and demanded Putin immediately pull his troops out of Ukraine.

Wallace explained that he thought the motion was actually 'important and necessary', as it 'correctly condemns Russian aggression and calls for humanitarian support for Ukraine and Ukrainian refugees'.

But he said he couldn't support it because other aspects of it evidenced how the EU was 'manipulating public anger to accelerate militarisation'. He also said that he was acting 'in the tradition of Irish neutrality and international support for peace' and had been elected on a platform of opposing war.

If the failure of the right of European politics in respect of Russia can be seen in the manner in which former prime ministers of various European countries (France, Finland and Italy) have enriched themselves on the boards of Russian companies, the failure of the left can be seen in the posturing and the theoretical arguments offered by those who pose as tribunes of the people.

In an article in *The Irish Times* which was an attempt to clarify the logic of his vote, Wallace (in tandem with Clare Daly, another Irish MEP who voted as Wallace did) again condemned the Russian invasion but wrote also: 'Although Russia alone invaded Ukraine, both Russia and the West bear responsibility for creating conditions of instability and confrontation in Ukraine, in pursuit of their strategic and economic interests. ... The country has been used as a pawn.'

Context is everything here. And the context of that vote by Wallace was that it came on an emotional day when Ukrainian president, Volodymyr Zelenskyy, got a standing ovation following an address to the European Parliament by online link from a city that was under bombardment from Putin's army.

Did it not matter to Wallace what Zelenskyy asked for or what the Ukrainian people might want? It is notable that in a newspaper defence of their vote, Wallace and Daly did not see fit to mention Zelenskyy's appearance or the words that he spoke in the parliament in which they sit.

Another context is that of death, including death on a soccer field. This is something that can be understood wherever you are in the world. Just as sport is relatable, so are love and grief. Among the cascade of horrendous news that has filled our screens over the past fortnight is the story of a sixteen-year-old boy, Iliya, who died in Ukraine in the first days of war.

He was playing soccer in the Ukrainian city of Mariupol when the Russians started shelling the city. He was caught on the field in the shelling and hit. He was rushed to hospital but died on the operating table, the surgeons unable to save him.

The truth of this war can be heard in the wail of grief that filled the hospital. Iliya's father, identified only as Serhii in news reports, held his son's dead body through a sheet and hugged his head, convulsed with grief.

Held fast by their ideological straitjacket, the attempts of Wallace and Daly to explain their position on Ukraine became increasingly absurd. Abstractions offer no defence for moral failures; and sport offers absolutely no guarantee of basic ethics.

## Morality and Sporting Administrators

The moral bankruptcy of too many sporting administrators has been revealed time and again. Some have had their snout in the trough, while others have demonstrated a capacity to facilitate political regimes that act in inexcusable ways.

The manner in which sporting organisations have disgraced themselves with their identification with Vladimir Putin is just one more example of their failures of judgement. It has happened across the history of these organisations, most notoriously with Hitler and the Berlin Games of 1936. But it has also happened in countries great and small – from the Olympian cavorting with the Chinese in recent decades to the Argentinian junta's World Cup of 1978.

When I teach this aspect of modern sports history to my students in UCD, I use the work of the French sociologist and philosopher, Jean-Marie Brohm, who taught for many decades at the University of Montpellier. Since the late 1960s, Brohm repeatedly set out the manifold failures in the world of sport, most brilliantly doing so in his recent book, *La Tyrannie sportive: Théorie critique d'un opium du peuple.*

Brohm argues that the modern spectacle of sport 'treats the masses as morons', 'that any hope of "cleaning up sport" financially speaking is an illusion', that it 'enslaves women and perpetuates the patriarchal system', that sport serves the function of inducing people to 'to acclaim the established social-political system'.

Almost invariably, students agree with Brohm's analysis of the ills of sport. They cannot argue against the weight of evidence that demonstrates the sordid aspect of the modern sporting world.

Where they almost always disagree with Brohm, though, is in respect of the action he calls for. Brohm has called, time and again, for the boycotting of Olympic Games, World Cups and all of those vast modern sporting events that dominate huge swathes of modern media. He argues, simply, that modern 'sport must be smashed'.

But the students – representative of wider society – really enjoy sporting festivals and particularly enjoy them when there is Irish participation, notably when that participation includes at least some success.

This is the great conundrum: on the one hand, modern sport is run by organisations whose basic capacity for ethical behaviour has repeatedly been shown to be appalling. But, on the other hand, major sporting occasions lend drama and colour and joy to hundreds of millions of people from every section of society all across the world.

Vladimir Putin has used the world of sport as his plaything. He has sought Russian success in international competition as a matter of national prestige. And he has used major sporting events in seeking to demonstrate that Russia is a modern, normal state.

To achieve this, Russian money and influence went to work on those who run world sport. What emerged was the grotesque spectacle of pretence that there was nothing to see beyond the boundaries of sporting contests; that sport and sportspeople were somehow entitled to choose to live in a world where Putinism did not matter or even really exist.

The highpoints of his success in this were the Sochi Winter Olympics of 2014 and the FIFA World Cup of 2018. In sporting terms, both were brilliantly run, hugely successful sporting competitions. But they were also the centrepiece of a massive propaganda drive by Putin.

To be clear, by the time of their stagings, that Putin was a murderous tyrant was not in doubt. The litany of the misdeeds of his regime was well-established. Opponents had been murdered or posoined or had 'taken their own lives'; he had started a short, brutal war with Georgia (2008); he annexed Ukraine's Crimea region in 2014; and then fomented war in eastern Ukraine in that same year which left thousands dead.

Basically, there was repeated, demonstrable evidence of the scale of his brutality; all the while, he extended his own wealth and power, creating a privileged elite around him, suborning the state to his ambitions.

When FIFA awarded the 2018 World Cup to Russia, Putin said: 'The decision shows that Russia is trusted.' The staging on 15 July 2018 of the World Cup final in Moscow saw Putin bask in the immediate glow of what was widely considered to be a brilliant tournament. By the time of the 2018 FIFA World Cup, such legitimacy was conferred on Russia through sport that there were repeated testimonies offered of how the country was not at all like it was portrayed to be in the western media. Indeed, at the time, the BBC reported the broad consensus that the World Cup was a 'resounding public relations success'. This was neatly encapsulated in the words of one England supporter, who gave his name as Darren from Blackpool: 'Everything the British government has said about Russia is a lie. It's propaganda. Fair play to Putin. He's done a brilliant job with the World Cup.'

This is exactly what the men who run FIFA thought, also.

It was not just a soccer tournament, of course; it was also the centrepiece of a massive propaganda drive by Putin. The mission was to use sport to project his own importance and, all the while, deflect attention from the imperialist violence that had sat at the heart of his regime for almost two decades. In all of this, the two most important sporting bodies in the world – the International Olympic Council and FIFA – were in his corner. It says much that FIFA's president Gianni Infantino (also a member of the International Olympic Council) still declines to return the Russian Order of Friendship Medal bestowed on him by Putin. As he told Putin in Moscow: 'We are a team.'

The Irish have not been innocent bystanders in all of this.

The Irish mixed martial arts fighter Conor McGregor was invited to the 2018 FIFA World Cup as Putin's guest. He posed with Putin, had a photo taken with his arm around Putin's shoulders and posted pictures on Instagram where he described Putin in fawning terms. He wrote: 'Today I was invited to the World Cup final as a guest of Russian president Vladimir Putin. This man is one of the greatest leaders of our time and I was honored to attend such a landmark event alongside him. Today was an honor for me Mr. Putin. Thank you and congratulations on an amazing World Cup. Россия вперёд (Go Russia!)'

The post received more than 3,100,000 likes.

For his part, Pat Hickey – for so long the central person in the Olympic movement in Ireland – sat beside Putin at the Olympic Games and at the European Games in Baku. Their shared love of judo helped forge a connection that drew them together. Hickey has said of his relationship with Putin: 'He's the patron of the Judo Federation in Russia and the World Judo Federation and I meet him at tournaments. He is not an honorary black belt – he's a fighting black belt. We'd talk about the stars of judo … That relationship built up between us. So any time I was in Russia on business, I invariably got an invitation to come and see him in the Kremlin. I had the privilege of being twice there to see him, once to have dinner with him but not just us on our own, there were about five or six other people, which was a great honour and great privilege.'

War in Ukraine is rooted in that historical claim Putin made and remade in the days before he invaded, when he described Ukraine as not a real country and Ukrainians as not a real people. That is the language of fascism. It is founded on the warp of history that Putin has constructed.

The construction of that warp, of the conditions that allowed Putin to act as he has, of the brutal reality of his power had many accomplices. Among them are the sporting administrators of FIFA and the IOC.

# 17 ENDGAME

The past is constantly pushed to one side to make room for the future. In *The Rings of Saturn*, W.G. Sebald wrote about the transience of all things human, not just individual lives, but also whole families, buildings, communities, towns, ideas, ways of life, love, friendship and everything else. He wrote: 'On every new thing there lies already the shadow of annihilation. For the history of every individual, of every social order, indeed of the whole world, does not describe an ever-widening, more and more wonderful arc, but rather follows a course which, once the meridian is reached, leads without fail into the dark.' Sebald's vision holds true for sport, where the only certainty is change. No sport can stand still and imagine that its present status is enough to guarantee its future. The world of sport itself is all the time subject to the shifts in the organisation of wider society. In the modern world, the ubiquity of sports – and the power of the organisations that run sport – is manifest most potently in the sports grounds that proliferate. There is something deeply impressive about a well-made sports stadium, one that is unique and fitted into its environment in a way that augments itself and everything around it. While it stands, there are few better places to understand the life of a city. The illusion is that – because it is built of bricks and mortar – it will last forever, but of course it is built unto the moment and its time will pass, just as surely as did that of the Colosseum in Rome.

## Gaming

The rise and rise of video games is a truly unique aspect of modern popular culture. If anyone doubts just how deep of a hold it takes on its devotees, they would do well to read Simon Parkin's brilliant book *Death by Video Game: Tales of Obsession from the Virtual Frontline*.

Parkin has written extensively about video game culture in publications such as *The New Yorker* and *New Scientist*, and in this book he explores what it is that makes video games so attractive.

As the title of the book suggests, this is an attraction that lures people to their deaths. There are many recent examples of people dying during long sessions of playing video games, in arcades or internet cafés or at home on their consoles.

Among the more extreme examples is the 2012 story of twenty-three-year-old Chen Rong-Yu who went into an internet café in New Taipei City in Taiwan and logged onto the hugely popular game *League of Legends*. Over the following twenty-three hours, he played and played, stopping only to rest his head on the desk in front of him to sleep in brief snatches.

On the last occasion that he lay his head on the table, he remained unmoving for nine hours until he was approached by a person who worked in the café – but he was, by then, already dead.

This was one of a series of fatalities – particularly in the gaming halls of East Asia – that have taken place over the past five years, but this catalogue of death is nothing new, and nor is it peculiar to that region.

For example, as far back as 1982, in Illinois, an eighteen-year old gamer – a brilliant young student who had plans to study medicine – fell dead after recording a record high score on the arcade game *Berserk*.

Now, people die playing all manner of sports every year, but the deaths of gamers lend themselves to a very particular idea – the notion that this loss of life is confirmation that gaming is a particularly useless way to spend your days.

Indeed, since their emergence from the computer research projects of America's universities and institutes, video games have always been looked down on as a complete waste of time by those who frown on their relentless growth in popularity. From the first arcade games, the rise of *Space Invaders* and *Pac-Man*, the growth of Atari home systems and on to the phenomenal success of Xbox and PlayStation, there can be no denying that this virtual world of play is defying its critics and will surely continue to do so.

Those critics dismiss video games as not being a suitable way to pass time. Its greatest defects are presented as being a failure to properly stimulate either the body or the mind. For example, it is considered to be in no way as wholesome as the fresh air and exercise central to ball games or the mind-expanding joy of reading books.

Indeed, as Simon Parkin wrote, they are seen instead as impoverished or depraved or infantile. The image of the video gamer sitting almost motionless apart from the repeated twitching of their thumbs, transfixed by a screen, faces contorted by intent is one of the great emblematic images in the minds of those who decry all that is wrong in modern popular culture. Indeed, it is an image which reinforces the worst aspects of the loneliness and antisocial strains of the modern world.

People have feared the impact of video games from the very beginning. In fact, in the 1980s, the British House of Commons almost introduced punitive legislation which would have dramatically curbed the capacity of those who wished to play them. At the same time police in England actually claimed that the phenomenon of playing *Space Invaders* had doubled the amount of house break-ins in the south of England.

Much worse than that, it is routinely claimed – usually with the most unimpressive of evidence – that violent video games are the cause of multiple shootings either by the delusions fostered in shooters or in the training they are purported to offer to those who wish to commit crimes.

But in depicting video games in this manner, critics are missing the positives that those who love to game point to as among the benefits that can accrue. Research shows that video games can 'improve hand-eye co-ordination, cognitive flexibility, decision making and even vision. Video games are increasingly sociable and inclusive. And, at the philosophical level, play does, of course, educate and prepare us for usefulness in the world.'

More than that, video games also offer an unparalleled escape from the realities of life. The joy of escapism is central to a happy life. And if video games provide and escape from the intolerable, the distressing or simply from the mundane, then how can they be so roundly condemned?

What is plain is that video games are loved by many; they are an essential part of popular culture; their development continues to attract more and more players every year. The instinct to dismiss this play as not constituting real sport is understandable, but the boundaries have shifted and will shift again.

## The Future of Sport

Imagining the future of sport hinges on three basic questions:

a) What do we mean by 'sport'?
b) Will there always be sport?
c) What will sport be?

Before attempting any prediction of the future, the need for a certain realism must be acknowledged. The Irish story of soccer, alone, is a reminder that it is not easy to read the sporting future. There are two instances – more than a century apart – which demonstrate the challenge. In the first instance, the Belfast businessman, John McAlery, brought two Scottish teams (Queen's Park and Caledonian) to Belfast on 24 October 1878 to play an exhibition match in the hope of making some money and more broadly to help establish soccer in Ireland. A good crowd turned out for the match and it is noted as a landmark event in the spread of the game of soccer to Ireland – and then across Ireland. But a journalist covering that first match sneered at the players who went around 'butting at the ball like a pack of young goats' and predicted that soccer would never take off in Ireland. Then, just over a century later in 1989, in the aftermath of the Irish international team making progress at Euro '88 and then in the qualifying campaign for Italia '90, the RTÉ broadcaster John Bowman wrote in *The Sunday Times* that it was naïve to imagine that soccer, rugby and Gaelic football could all prosper indefinitely on such a small island: 'Many astute observers reckon that the threat must be to Gaelic football.' In *The Irish Times*, Michael Finlan agreed: 'We do seem to have reached the stage where soccer, a once-reviled symbol of foreign yokes and repression, is threatening to become the national game of Ireland.' Both men were wrong, with Gaelic football and then rugby enjoying the most prosperous decades in their history, even if there was a logic to their speculation.

\* \* \*

There is the inevitable academic debate on how precisely sport should be defined; it is also irredeemably tedious. This is partly because there is no straightforward answer to the apparently simple question: what is meant by 'sport'? What we in a new millennium consider to be 'sport' is different to that of past generations of Irish people. There was a time, several centuries ago, when the word 'sport' was almost fully centred on the world of hunting. This has entirely changed.

There are now definitions of sport that include board games. For example, since 1930 Ireland has hosted the European Ludo championships six times and the world championships twice.

Ultimately, the answer lies in subjective choice. While all of us may accept that athletics or the various football and stick-and-ball games are sport, deciding where the margins lie is ultimately a matter of personal taste. So, in your opinion, is hunting a sport? Or chess? Or darts? Or synchronised swimming? Or gaming? Valid arguments can be made either way. But wherever one chooses to draw the line, within its boundaries there is a vast array of sport. Indeed, there are now small libraries of books and reports that bear relentless witness to the sheer diversity of modern sport.

The difficulties in defining where the sporting world begins and ends become even more acute whenever you move beyond the mainstream that dominates the sporting media in the western world. For example, Andrew Keh has documented the weird and wonderful world of Finnish sport. It is true that mainstream sport thrives in Finland, where ice hockey, motor sport, soccer and athletics are all hugely popular. But there is another sporting world which is gloriously strange. Finland is home, for example, to the Wife Carrying World Championship (the winner receives the weight of the wife in beer), the Mobile Phone Throwing World Championship (Finland is the home of Nokia) and the Air Guitar World Championship ('It's not what you play, it's how you play it'). The World Sauna Championships were held in Finland for more than a decade until they were abandoned in 2010 when one of the competitors – a

Russian named Vladimir Ladyzhensky – died of third-degree burns. Then there are the fifty acres of swamp that host the Swamp Soccer Championships. This swamp – near the town of Hyrynsalmi – has hosted the championship which now draws 200 teams who play six-a-side matches.

The story of sport in Ireland is similarly diverse. The major field games, horse racing and other mainstream sports may dominate, but every year, an enormous variety of popular pastimes lives and breathes beyond the suffocation of the dominant sports. From tug-o'-war to churn-rolling, the passion for fun and for competition – mixed in whatever weightings as suit the individual – offers something a little different.

As well as accepting the need for being flexible in defining sport, what must also be accepted is that sport is much more than elite athletes competing in formally organised or professionalised environments. That is obviously one type of sport, but what makes the world of sport so powerful is its hinterland: that vast swathe of people who love play and who feel a connection to an elite athlete because they, too, play a game, watch a game, love a game. Ultimately, the scale of what is encapsulated in the meaning of 'sport' – and understanding also that this meaning changes all the time – sets the frame for attempting to imagine the future.

\* \* \*

Sport – in some form or other – will continue to be central to modern life for the imaginable future. The logic of this is straightforward. Every society for which we have meaningful evidence holds evidence of sport; there is no sense that this is about to change in any foreseeable future. The history of Ireland is a case in point. People on the island played sport century after century. Within this history, there are aspects of Ireland's sporting past that are uniquely Irish and are defined by the peculiarities of a small island on the edge of Europe. What is equally apparent, however, is that the Irish sporting world is unique only in parts; there is much of the history of Irish sport that is a shared history with that of other societies, near and far. This is partly a reflection of the universal instincts that draw humans to the idea of play, partly a reflection of the history of Ireland within what was once the British Empire, and partly, also, a reflection of an international cultural exchange where political and geographic borders are permeable.

Sport has been transformed over time, particularly over the past 150 years; modern sport is often big business and it often, too, has a political function. The manner in which sport is continuously repackaged – not least by modern media – creates the illusion of constant change. And yet, the story of sport is, at least in part, the story of people finding new ways of doing the same thing. A primal passion for play underpins any understanding of the origins and development of the modern sporting world. And it underpins, also, the sense that sport is so fundamental to people that it appears inconceivable that it will not continue in one form or another.

There is no end to the array of statistics that set out the importance of sport to modern society. These statistics – compiled by states and sporting organisations and research institutes and businesses – document virtually every aspect of the modern sporting world. From the percentage of the global population who play and watch sport to the centrality of sporting events and sports merchandising to the economy, the evidence of how our world is soaked in sport is undeniable.

There is another way to consider this question of whether there will always be sport. During the initial stages of the lockdowns during the Covid-crisis we got something of an insight into what a world without sport might look like. The first way in which the impact of the loss of sporting activity was made apparent was in the loss of the physical act of play. The happiness of a lot of homes rests on the rhythm of playing and training and playing and training. This is true for adults, and especially true for children. Channelling play into a framework of competition is the essence of modern sport. And the loss of that framework rendered clear just how valuable a function it serves as a part of so many lives.

But play is only part of the story of the centrality of sport, the second aspect is the social life that is wrapped around that play. At the core of this is the idea of 'the day out'. Communal gatherings around sport events are a vital part of our world. The role of the sports club in modern society is readily apparent. In such clubs, people love and fight and do all the things that people do whenever they come together, for good or for ill. Clubs being shut for training and matches means much more than just the loss of physical release, it also means the loss of a social outlet that sits at the core of many lives. About 120 years ago, a Glentoran soccer player who attempted to explain why he had disappeared for four weeks to play soccer in Glasgow when he should have been playing in Belfast, said simply: 'I did not go away. I got drunk and found myself in Glasgow.' The social aspect of sport is not normally quite as dramatic as that – but short of ending up in Glasgow for a month, there is still a lot of fun associated with sport.

\* \* \*

If we then accept that sport will continue into the foreseeable future, what forms will it take, what will sport look like? We must begin by acknowledging that traditions of play are also vital. A lot of what we might believe to be change is actually no more substantial than window dressing. Such change does not simply obliterate old traditions; instead, it often built on those traditions, refashioning them for a new age. The great Irish example of this is the game we know as hurling. The physical evidence of a stick and ball game played on this island extends back to the medieval world. A hurling ball in the National Museum of Ireland that has been carbon-dated to the second half of the twelfth century lends further credence to the claimed antiquity of hurling, as revealed in Clodagh Doyle's exhibition *Hair Hurling Balls – Earliest Artefacts of Our National Game*. This exhibition centres on fourteen hurling balls that have been discovered in Irish bogs by people cutting turf. The balls were discovered as far north as Sligo and as far south as Kerry. Carbon-dating places the balls in every century from the twelfth through to the end of the seventeenth century. This suggests a continuity of human endeavour that was carried on as the game grew in the eighteenth century and then adopted its modern form with the founding of the GAA. References to the game in written texts extend the history of play both further into the past and deeper into society. The simple point to make is that across centuries of colonisation, immense cultural change, plague, war and famines, people continued to hit a ball with a stick in Ireland. The simple point is that it is not just that history suggests that people will continue to play, it also suggests that they will continue to play particular activities. As well as hurling, the long record of sporting activities in Ireland documents centuries of kicking a football, racing each other, racing horses, engaging in feats of endurance, and other familiar acts of skill and strength.

\* \* \*

The history of sport has been changed and changed again by technological innovations. The nineteenth century construction of national sporting cultures was made possible only by the invention of the steam engine and the rapid construction of a rail network. During the mid-nineteenth century there was a reaction against 'the monstrosity and evils of steam engines' that were perceived to be re-ordering society, but in that re-ordering sport immediately prospered. Trains brought people to all manner of popular spectacles. This included – in the 1840s in England – special excursion trains to public hangings, but more prosaically the scheduling of 'bare-knuckle boxing trains', the facilitation of participation in hunting, the establishment of a truly national calendar of horseracing, and – ultimately – of the development of cup and league competitions in newly-invented field games as the nineteenth century progressed. Firstly through travel on steam-powered ships and then on planes, national sporting cultures evolved into international ones; the revolution in transport made possible the construction of a world of play that would previously have been beyond reach. Engines annihilated the meaning of distance; the leap from horse to jet remade the boundaries of sporting competition.

Other inventions were also vital; this is true not just of the invention itself but also the process by which such inventions were commercialised. For example, the technological advance of the bicycle between the 1860s and 1880s was exceptionally rapid and led to the production of bikes which had light, tubular frames, suspension wheels and solid rubber tyres. But as well as the modern bicycle itself, what was also vital was the system of mass-production that allowed for the cycling craze and the attendant sporting competition that was an off-shoot of that craze. Similarly, the development of cups and leagues at all level of games – from soccer and rugby to American football and tennis – would not have been possible without the mass-production of standardised balls. Goodyear's vulcanised rubber – and the bladders which were inflated beneath the leather panels of footballs – were an essential step in the development of modern sport.

\* \* \*

The internet is the latest technological invention to transform sport; we are only at the beginning of the change that it is bringing to how sport is organised. It is not that traditional sporting activities will be destroyed by this process, but they will be changed. This is inevitable. The reach of the internet is transforming our world in so many different ways. From shopping to social life, and from gaming to celebrity culture, there is nothing that has not felt the insistent press of its influence. It is having a profound impact on human behaviours. Take, for instance, the growth of social media. It is a self-evident truth that it has changed how people live with each other. To believe that sports will stand removed from this process is not realistic.

The sheer scale of the reach of social media grows by the day and is stunning. A report produced in Vancouver last year by two media companies, Hootsuite and We Are Social, entitled 'Digital 2020', laid bare in raw numbers digital trends and popular engagement with social media. This report showed how more than 4.5 billion people are now online – with almost 300 million new internet users joining in 2019 alone. The report also showed how almost half of the world's population (close to four billion people) now use social media. This was an increase of 9 per cent (amounting to more than 321 million people) from the previous year. The basic point is that those who remain offline – 'The Unconnected' – are now a minority, and their numbers are growing fewer every day. More than that, the average internet user around the world will spend more than 100 days of the year online, if you count up all the hours that they clock up. More than one-third of that time is spent on social media – some two hours and thirty minutes.

Sport is an essential part of this process; it provides much of the content, in one form or another. The television revolution of the past fifty years saw sport become a central feature of modern broadcasting. Where once sporting events on television were occasional treats sparsely sprinkled across the schedule, by the new millennium they were central to mainstream programming, as well as having a growing number of channels dedicated to their coverage. The omnipresence of sport in the media, combined with the rapidly expanding sports applications available on various devices from computers to smartphones, is the ultimate example of the triumph of sport: there is now no event, regardless of how small and insignificant it might appear to others, that cannot be made accessible across the world using the internet.

The globalisation of modern sports, which began with international touring teams in various sports and deepened with the organisation of Olympic Games and then World Cups in multiple sports, has quickened and assumed new forms through the internet. The spread of American commercialised sport is a prime example of this. In the introduction to a report published in 2020 on the future of sport, Jeremy Jacobs, the chairman of Delaware North, the company that owns the Boston Bruins ice hockey team, said: 'These are critical years, as franchises and leagues compete for international attention and seek to build ties with fans who live thousands of miles away. It is time to start thinking of the entire globe as our hometown market.' This is a process that is already well underway. It can be seen in the steady advance of the popularity of American sports for more than 100 years. American influence saw baseball, for example, adopted with great passion in Cuba and in Japan in the late nineteenth century. As the decades passed, baseball was joined by American football and – especially – by basketball. This sport – invented in America in the 1890s – has proven America's great gift to the world of sport.

The spread of American sports has been a process driven by commercialisation. Nowhere in the world are sporting entrepreneurs as successful as they are in America. Its sports professionalised early and the scale of the continent offered enormous wealth to those who could harness the love of sport. This extended to exporting sport to wherever people might pay gate money. For example, the idea of racing dogs around an enclosed track in pursuit of an electric hare spread from America across Britain and Ireland in the 1920s; it was adopted with immediate and considerable relish. In 1927, tracks were opened in Dublin (10,000 people were thought to have attended the opening night at Shelbourne Park), Belfast and Cork. These were quickly followed by tracks at Limerick and Waterford. Huge crowds came to the races, drawn by the excitement of watching dogs race under lights and drawn, too, by the opportunity to gamble.

A more recent example centres on the growth of basketball and the various ways in which it has thrived in Ireland. The erection of basketball hoops in city playgrounds, in schoolyards and, ultimately, to the walls of family houses has allowed for everything from pick-up games to one-on-one to solitary shooting. Beyond that again there are school leagues and the growth of basketball clubs in towns and cities. Finally, there was the establishment of a Irish national basketball league. In the 1980s, this was a thoroughly glamorous affair where imported Americans lived as cult heroes in communities such as the northsides of Cork and Dublin cities, in Belfast, and in the country towns of Tralee and Ballina. The league lost its sheen over time, but its heyday was a thing of great splendour and a reminder of the potential of sport to change people's lives – even momentarily – by exposing them to something new.

Naturally, the wider growth of American popular culture as a global phenomenon was central to all of this. American music, American films, American television all promoted the idea of its sports to the point where they became familiar and desirable. The broadcast of American football on Irish television from the 1980s showed again how sporting cultures can be remade in new places as a form of entertainment. It was not that it was expected that there would be American football clubs established in every corner of the land – but identification with the sport certainly helped with sponsorship deals and with the sale of merchandise to people who could recognise and identify with brands through sport.

\*\*\*

There is nothing new about empires spreading their sports across the world – the globalisation of sport is not in any way a new thing. Every significant empire has brought its sports to the boundaries of its realm. You can see that through the building of Roman colosseums and amphitheatres at El Jem in Tunisia or at Pula in Croatia or at Chester in England.

It was in these spaces that the Romans staged gladiatorial games and wrestling matches and cockfights. In the east – in the early modern period – the Mughals spread polo, just as Chinese dynasties had done before them. And later, in the nineteenth century, the English took a modern version of that game and spread it for their elite across their empire. Their polo was part of the wider sporting life of the British Empire – they also built race-tracks and cricket pitches, and put up goalposts, almost everywhere they went.

Will the power and gathering prestige of China transform the sports that people play, or the manner in which they play them? Similarly, what about the sheer scale and increasing wealth of India? Already, the Indian Premier League (IPL) – founded in 2007 – has transformed the game of cricket in a way that has reached into other sports. For example, the league generates billions of euros on an annual basis, primarily to the Indian economy. It has also added new ancillary businesses, in a mass way, to the traditional revenue streams of gate receipts, sponsorship, merchandising and media rights. The use of new media – for example, the pioneering use of YouTube – has been powerfully exploited, as has the development of fantasy sports and sportsbook betting, drawing in hundreds of millions of fans. The short-form of cricket that is played in the league, the manner in which it is organised with player auctions, and other innovations have provided content that attracts and holds the interest of the public. The scale of the entertainment is perfectly pitched as a product for a new internet age – a traditional game remade for a digital world, drawing at ease from both aspects of past and present.

What it also clear is that the reach of American sports has accelerated in the new millennium. This is an acceleration that is facilitated by the internet. Having a smartphone, or a laptop, or a tablet of some description, allows you to watch any National Basketball Association, National Football League or Major League Baseball match. You don't need a television and don't need to depend on what a broadcaster chooses to show you. No matter where you are in the world, if you are on the internet you can watch every match live and in full, and are not dependent on television stations to broadcast them. More than that, entire matches sit on the websites and can be watched again in full. As the sports broadcasting market increasingly splinters into ever more slender pieces, this revolution in broadcasting offers a direct route from sporting organisations to fans, and presents the possibility of huge sums being paid by way of subscription. The sheer scale of American sports and the extent of their existing commercialisation offer them a massive advantage as they seek to extend their sphere of influence. And where American broadcasting of sport goes, the rest of the world follows.

\* \* \*

But the internet is doing much more than changing how the world engages with traditional sports; it has also nurtured a whole new sphere of sporting activity. The great transformation of the new millennium is the growth of esports – short for electronic sports. A huge variety of such games exist, including *League of Legends, Mortal Kombat,*

*FIFA*, *Overwatch*, *Heroes of the Storm*, *Fortnite*, *NBA2K20* and *Call of Duty*, falling into the broad categories of strategy games, shooters, and sport and race simulations.

By 2017 video game play was the leading consumer-entertainment industry in the world – larger than both the film and music industries. This vast hinterland of amateur players is the mass from which an elite of players has emerged to win fame and riches. These players compete in esports competitions, which are organised as a spectator sport, involving professional contestants and watched by viewers online or on television. Professional esports players make their money from tournament winnings, as well as from sponsors and live-streaming revenue.

By 2020, more than 150 million people were watching esports events each month and the industry was valued at more than €1 billion. The industry is driven by Asia, with the western world now following rapidly. The extent of the change is made apparent by the development of esports programmes in American universities and high schools. The inclusion of esports in the 2018 Asian Games – and the success of that inclusion – demonstrates just how far the discipline has come in a very short space of time. Ultimately, esports will take their place in the Olympic Games. Those who doubt this should be the case should consider that for the 2020 Tokyo Olympics, skateboarding – to give just one example of a sport that moved mainstream from the margins – was sanctioned as an Olympic sport. The alternative is that esports avoid the formal structures of the modern sporting organisations that constitute the Olympic movement and its sports. That, in itself, would mark a rejection of the sporting traditions of the mainstream and would constitute a massive shift in the organisation of sport.

\* \* \*

The internet is only one aspect of technological change that will matter in the coming years. Coaching will be transformed by in-play communication with players, in much the same way as Formula 1 drivers are communicated with by team leaders. High-tech playing surfaces will allow for incrementally improved performance, as will enhanced equipment and playing gear. Evolution in knowledge of nutrition and hydration will similarly lead to incremental gains. In general, the ongoing medicalisation of sporting performance will also be essential to the success of any competitor as new insights are used to condition physical performance. Games will also be transformed by medical knowledge in a different manner in that awareness of the adverse impact of sporting actions, notably collisions, will lead to the revision of playing rules; this will most likely lead to a ban on heading a ball as well as severe restrictions on the nature of tackling.

The impact of artificial intelligence (AI) is likely to be immense. Advances in computer power and in the gathering and usage of data, with the possibilities for enhanced cognitive abilities in machines, will undoubtedly change many aspects of sport. It will obviously impact on the business of sport by allowing unprecedented insight into consumer behaviour and personalised marketing. It should lead to better officiating, with a sport such as boxing ripe for more accurate judging.

The more significant question is the extent to which AI will be applied to sporting performance. One of the great challenges in sport is how to use information, how to sift through evidence, prioritise that which is considered most relevant and use this as an aid to enhance performance. The logic of AI is that it should allow an increasingly information-based approach to such matters as pre- and post-match analysis of both teams and their opponents. For example, AI – properly harnessed – will help teams understand patterns of play used by their opponents. And in terms of preparing players, workouts will increasingly be personalised and managed through real-time information feedback to improve both technique and efficacy of effort. The bottom line in all of this is not just accuracy of information, but also accuracy of analysis and accuracy of application.

The great unknowable is the extent to which AI will play against the undeniable emotional aspect of sport. Will human behaviour be so fundamentally changed by AI that emotional actions and reactions will be overwhelmed? And even if not overwhelmed, to what extent will they be tempered? It will be fascinating to watch how this unfolds; emotion is fundamental to the meaning of sport, to the connections between participant and spectator, to the drama that unfolds. Any significant loss of emotion will diminish the experience and the spectacle.

\* \* \*

Much of the emotion in sport flows from the relationship between sport and identity. This works on multiple levels.

Personal identity, local identity and national identity are prisms through which sporting activity is considered. The cornerstone of the modern sporting world is the rulebook by which organisations legislate for their games. On a practical basis, disputes over the rules of play are contentious and divisive. But no disputes are quite as brutal as ones fought around identity. Ordinarily, these are disputes that extend far beyond sport and often into wider society. People who believe that their identities are being denied to them or in someway infringed upon are often genuinely aggrieved, whether it be in relation to gender or nationality, for example. And yet there are many others who are more than happy to use rulebooks in a way which allows them to make any compromise around identity – particularly national identity – that allows them or their team to be successful. In this regard, sportspeople have long accepted the notion of redrawing the boundaries of nationality whenever it suits. In a world where migration is set to continue on an epic scale, the idea of international sport as a contest between nations will continue to lose much of its conviction.

In general, disputes over identity will most certainly extend into the future. Sport will continue to be used as a platform by athletes who wish for social justice and who can conceive of sport as a vehicle to facilitate change in wider society. This will be revealed in campaigns for racial justice and also in the gathering conflict around the place of transgender athletes in the sporting world. This is a new variation on a longstanding issue; since the 1930s, mechanisms to define 'femaleness' have been used to define eligibility for women's sport. As most prominently illustrated in the case of the South African runner, Caster Semenya, the most recent approach has focused on testosterone. The natural occurrence of elevated testosterone levels in women such as Semenya has led to the insistence by World Athletics that testosterone be suppressed to allow the athlete in question to compete in women's events. A future expansion of this practice to include intersex and transgender athletes will almost certainly create deep and ongoing controversy.

\*\*\*

In all of this, the manner in which global society is changing will impact on sport in ways that we do not yet appreciate. Rapid urbanisation is a prime example. The United Nations note that some 1.5 million people are added to the world's cities every week. This urbanisation is – in large part – driven by population growth. Indeed, the estimates are that some two-thirds of the estimated nine billion people on the planet in 2050 will be living in cities. How will international sport, currently largely organised on a nation–state basis, manage in this context? Will there be a greater shift to global competitions between clubs which represent cities? The search for rapid economic growth, the cycles of boom and bust, the vast income disparity and the dislocation that flows from it, are also important. Where does sport fit into this pursuit for wealth and the power that flows from economic growth? What will be the sporting tastes and patterns of consumption of this growing global population, and how will those tastes and patterns be shaped?

Given that population growth, urbanisation and increased economic activity are a formidable factor in climate change, the looming environmental crisis will inevitably shape the future of sport. As the temperature rises and resources of – for example – food and water become more pressurised, how will sporting bodies and event organisers meet the challenges of sustainability? No serious policy or strategy or vision for the future of sport can avoid this issue; it is clear that the context of wider environmental change will ultimately define much of how people play sport. A great example of this is the Winter Olympic Games. Such is the impact of greenhouse gases that just a little over half of the more than twenty cities that have hosted the Winter Olympics will be certain of being able to act as host by 2050. How does sport react to this? The installation of snow-making machines and of snow-farming might allow winter sports to survive, but there is an environmental cost in terms of the use of water and resources to allow this to happen, which exacerbates the problem that already exists. Sporting organisations have yet to seriously grapple with these issues.

\* \* \*

There is a thesis that the logical endpoint for the technological change that is underway will see humans replaced with robots, whose talents are refined, time and again, for enhanced performance. The ensuing sport would be entirely premised on entertainment, even voyeurism. Specifically developed robots already excel at such feats as throwing three-pointers in basketball and playing table tennis, to give two instances.

It is true that robots currently have a range of motion that is far behind even non-elite sports people. But it took some five decades of computer programming development before the supercomputer Deep Blue beat world chess champion Garry Kasparov in a game. The prospect of highly developed robots competing against each other in sporting events is a realistic one.

But while there is every likelihood that such a sporting world might be created, it will be to augment that which exists for humans, not to displace it. The love of play that drives sport sits at the heart of the human experience – just as it has across millennia. This love of play is something that is reinvented, again and again, to fit different societies in different places at different times. It seizes the mind as well as the body. And, ultimately, that is what will drive the future of sport.